Performance Windsurfing® with Mike Waltze

Performance

Windsurfing® with Mike Waltze

by Mike Waltze

with Phil Berman

Drawings by Steve Tonnesen

W · W · NORTON & COMPANY

New York　　　**London**

This book is dedicated to my parents,
who supported me in this sport,
even when it was thought to be "crazy."
and,
to the Schweitzer family,
who have done more for the sport of Windsurfing in the past few years
than anyone else could do in a lifetime.

MIKE WALTZE

Performance Windsurfing with Mike Waltze.

NOTE: Windsurfer® and Windsurfing® are trademarks of Windsurfer
International. Permission to use these terms here was
graciously granted by Windsurfing® International.
Copyright © 1985 by Mike Waltze and Phil Berman

Published simultaneously in Canada by Penguin Books Canada Ltd.,
2801 John Street, Markham, Ontario L3R 1B4.
Printed in Hong Kong by South China Printing Co.

The text of this book is composed in Trump Mediaeval, with
display type set in Inverserif Heavy Italic.
Book design by Jacques Chazaud

Library of Congress Cataloging in Publication Data

Waltze, Mike.
Performance Windsurfing with Mike Waltze.

1. Windsurfing.   I. Berman, Phil.   II. Title.
GV811.63.W56W36   1985   797.3'3   84-27218
ISBN 0-393-03301-5

W. W. Norton & Company, Inc., 500 Fifth Avenue, New York, N.Y. 10110
W. W. Norton & Company Ltd., 37 Great Russell Street, London WC1B 3NU

2 3 4 5 6 7 8 9 0

Contents

IV   CHOP JUMPING   81

V   WAVE JUMPING   94

VI   SURFING   117

VII   CHOOSING A BOARD AND FINS   142

VIII   SAILS AND OTHER GEAR   *161*

IX   SAFETY   *177*

Introduction

There comes a time for every sailboarder when he begins to wonder what it would be like to ride a performance board. His wonder is often accompanied with a tinge of jealousy, too. This is only natural. Watching a performance sailor go humming by from the deck of a standard twelve-foot sailboard is certainly intimidating and bound to incite a bit of envy.

I give plenty of credit to the sailor on a standard twelve-foot sailboard in moderate thirteen-knot winds and up. I say this because in stronger winds performance boards are not only more fun but actually easier to sail. Standard boards are designed for beginners, for freestyle and buoy racing, but are difficult to sail in solid breezes. This is why many who sail standard boards in high winds underestimate their own sailing abilities, just as a Cadillac driver at speed on a Grand Prix track might not realize how much easier it would be in a Porsche. In short, when the whitecaps start to show, it's time to put away that big board and hop on a performance board.

Proof that performance sailing is easier and more pleasurable than standard sailboarding in heavy air can be seen in the way my Hawaiian sailing friends react when I sail a standard board in a breeze to prepare for a race. They stare at me in awe, never failing to remind me that I'm just a bit of a fool. Why? Because most of them can't even begin to sail a standard board properly when winds are up. They know all too well that it's a punishing and often frustrating workout compared to carving jibes with ease and flying along on a reach with one hand dragging playfully in the water while hooked into the harness on a performance board.

Fred Haywood, who smashed three world speed records in 1983 for the fastest single-hulled sailboat, learned this the hard way. Back in 1981, when Fred had been sailing but two years in Maui, he and I used to race each other in local, twenty-knot-plus, tune-up races in preparation for events on the mainland. Since Fred had a lot less experience than I had at the time, I let Fred sail my Pan Am board with its fully retractable centerboard and high wind hullshape, while I raced him on a stock Windsurfer with a full daggerboard. My handicap evened out the competition a bit at first, but I knew that there would soon come a time when Fred would beat me, and I told myself

1

that when he did we would trade boards and then race again. Well, that day finally came. Fred whipped the pants off me. Naturally, Fred was jazzed up and proud of his well-earned victory. It was then that I knew Fred needed to have his ego deflated a bit, and so I said to Fred, "Okay, we're trading boards now." Fred left the beach on my Windsurfer feeling pretty confident that he'd at least give me a good fight. But Fred was in for a big surprise—he couldn't even make it to the weather mark! After circling the course on the Pan Am rig I met a dejected Fred on the beach. After thirty minutes or more of painful effort he had given up the fight. Fred learned that day that certain designs have a tremendous impact on performance. Having the right setup for any given type of wind and sea surface condition is the only way to go for maximum speed and pleasure. Perhaps it's no small wonder that Fred showed up for the speed trials at Weymouth, England, on a wing-masted sinker tuned and constructed especially for the highest of winds.

Performance boards are the way to go if you like to sail in solid breezes and/or the surf. When it's blowing over thirteen knots, the best word to describe performance sailing is effortless. Even so, a number of sailors I've met seem apprehensive about learning to sail a performance board. Whether this is because they've tried doing it when the wind was down or on poorly constructed or ill-matched equipment, gave up too soon, or

have never tried it, I can't say. What I can say is that if you purchase equipment that is suited to your needs and abilities, then sailing a performance board will be much easier than you may have imaged. In fact, if you are a persistent beginner, you can learn to sail a performance board in a matter of weeks. And if you already know how to sail a standard sailboard, the transition may only take a few days or, for some, just a few hours.

Performance boards are the best thing to happen to the sport since the harness and footstraps were invented. If winds are up, I always prefer sailing on a performance board. I get optimum speed from the wind, optimum height in my jumps, the sharpest and most powerful jibes, and the greatest thrill and challenge. All these pluses are what make performance sailing the natural progression for all enthusiastic windsurfers, whether they're sailing on a lake, in ocean swells, or in the surf.

You'll find as you read this book that it is loaded with information—some of which you may not be ready for. If this is the case, don't be afraid to skip over something and come back to it later, after you've gained more experience. It is my hope that you will find this book useful for a long time.

I hope also that the information here will serve as a steppingstone, leading you to the thrill, excitement, and adventures which I've enjoyed so much myself as a participant in the unique sport of windsurfing.

Mike Waltze

Mike Waltze is a pioneer in the sport of windsurfing, dating back to his first lesson in 1969 by inventor Hoyle Schweitzer on board and rig #12. Since that time, Mike has become a world champion in the racing, freestyle, and slalom aspects of the sport and has won a number of the renowned Maui Grand Prix and O'Neill wave riding and jumping events in Hawaii. Mike was on the forefront of the short board surfing era, innovating the development of the shorter, more maneuverable boards used today in high performance sailing. He is also the founder of Sailboards Maui Inc., known for its custom sailboard designs that have broken five world speed sailing records, the most noted of which is the 30.82-knot run by his partner, Fred Haywood, in Weymouth, England. Mike sails for Windsurfing International Inc., and collaborates on sail design for Neil Pryde. Mike currently lives on Maui, where he spends most of his time sailing, upgrading new designs for competition, and traveling to various events.

Phil Berman is a world champion Hobie Cat racer and one of the best-selling sailing writers in the world. He was the 1979 Hobie Cat-14 World Champion and second-place finisher in the 1981 Hobie Cat-18 Worlds. The author of several books and articles on sailing and a recent graduate of Harvard University, Phil lives in Santa Barbara, California, where he is a free-lance writer and educator.

Photo Credits

p. viii   Courtesy of *Windsurf Magazine*, Lou Perez
p. 3 (Intro)   Courtesy of *Windsurf Magazine*, Dan Merkel

Chapter 1

p. 6   Courtesy of *Windsurf Magazine*, by Craig Peterson
p. 8   Phil Berman
p. 9   Phil Berman
p. 10   Phil Berman
p. 11   Phil Berman
p. 13   Phil Berman
p. 14   Courtesy of *Windsurf Magazine*, by Craig Peterson

Chapter 2

p. 17   Courtesy of *Windsurf Magazine*, Dan Merkel
p. 18   Phil Berman
p. 19   Phil Berman
p. 20   Courtesy of *Windsurf Magazine*, by John Severson
p. 21   Courtesy of *Windsurf Magazine*, by John Severson
p. 22   Courtesy of *Windsurf Magazine*, by John Severson
p. 23   Courtesy of *Windsurf Magazine*, by John Severson
p. 24   Courtesy of *Windsurf Magazine*, by John Severson
p. 25   Courtesy of *Windsurf Magazine*, by John Severson
p. 27   Steve Wilkings
p. 29   Courtesy of *Windsurf Magazine*, by John Severson
p. 31   Courtesy of Hifly Sailboards
p. 32   Courtesy of Bic Sailboards
p. 33   Courtesy of Bic Sailboards
p. 34   Courtesy of Hifly Sailboards

Chapter 3

p. 40   Phil Berman
p. 41   Phil Berman
p. 43   Steve Wilkings
p. 44   Steve Wilkings
p. 45   Steve Wilkings
p. 46   Steve Wilkings
p. 47   Steve Wilkings
p. 49   Steve Wilkings
p. 50   Steve Wilkings
p. 51   Steve Wilkings
p. 52   Steve Wilkings
p. 53   Steve Wilkings
p. 55   Steve Wilkings
p. 56   Steve Wilkings
p. 57   Steve Wilkings
p. 58   Steve Wilkings
p. 59   Steve Wilkings
p. 60   Steve Wilkings
p. 61   Steve Wilkings
p. 63   Steve Wilkings
p. 64   Steve Wilkings
p. 65   Steve Wilkings
p. 66   Steve Wilkings
p. 67   Steve Wilkings
p. 68   Steve Wilkings
p. 69   Steve Wilkings
p. 71   Courtesy of *Windsurf Magazine*, by Jonathan Weston
p. 72   Courtesy of *Windsurf Magazine*, by Sylvain Cazenave
p. 73   Courtesy of *Windsurf Magazine*, by Sylvain Cazenave
p. 74   Steve Wilkings
p. 75   Steve Wilkings
p. 76   Steve Wilkings
p. 77   Steve Wilkings
p. 78   Steve Wilkings
p. 79   Steve Wilkings
p. 80   Steve Wilkings

Chapter 4

p. 83   Courtesy of *Windsurf Magazine*, by Steve Wilkings
p. 85   Courtesy of *Windsurf Magazine*, by John Severson
p. 86   Courtesy of *Windsurf Magazine*, by John Severson
p. 87   Courtesy of *Windsurf Magazine*, by John Severson
p. 88   Courtesy of *Windsurf Magazine*, by Darrell Wong
p. 89   Courtesy of *Windsurf Magazine*, by Darrell Wong
p. 90   Courtesy of *Windsurf Magazine*, by Darrell Wong
p. 91   Courtesy of Hifly Sailboards
p. 92   Courtesy of *Windsurf Magazine*, by John Severson

Chapter 5

p. 98   Courtesy of *Windsurf Magazine*, by John Severson
p. 99   Courtesy of *Windsurf Magazine*, by John Severson
p. 101   Courtesy of *Windsurf Magazine*, by John Severson
p. 102   Courtesy of *Windsurf Magazine*, by John Severson
p. 103   Courtesy of *Windsurf Magazine*, by John Severson
103 bottom   Phil Berman
p. 104   Courtesy of *Windsurf Magazine*, by John Severson
p. 105   Courtesy of *Windsurf Magazine*, by John Severson
p. 106   Courtesy of Hifly Sailboards
p. 108   Courtesy of *Windsurf Magazine*, by Steve Wilkings
p. 109   Courtesy of Hot Shots—Hawaii
p. 110   Courtesy of *Windsurf Magazine*, by John Severson
p. 111   Courtesy of *Windsurf Magazine*, by John Severson
p. 112   V. J. Lovero
p. 113   John Severson (5.16) and Angus Chater (5.17)
p. 115   Courtesy of *Windsurf Magazine*, by John Severson
p. 116   Courtesy of *Windsurf Magazine*, by Lou Perez

Chapter 6

p. 122   Courtesy of *Windsurf Magazine*, by John Severson
p. 123   Courtesy of *Windsurf Magazine*, by John Severson
p. 125   Courtesy of *Windsurf Magazine*, by Steve Wilkings
p. 126   Courtesy of *Windsurf Magazine*, by Dan Merkel
p. 127   Courtesy of *Windsurf Magazine*, by Dan Merkel
p. 128   Courtesy of *Windsurf Magazine*, by John Severson
p. 129   Courtesy of *Windsurf Magazine*, by John Severson
p. 130   Courtesy of *Windsurf Magazine*, by John Severson
p. 131   Courtesy of *Windsurf Magazine*, by Jonathan Weston
p. 132   Courtesy of *Windsurf Magazine*, by John Severson
p. 133   Courtesy of *Windsurf Magazine*, by John Severson
p. 134   Courtesy of *Windsurf Magazine*, by Steve Wilkings
p. 135   Courtesy of *Windsurf Magazine*, by John Severson
p. 136   Courtesy of *Windsurf Magazine*, by John Severson
p. 137   Courtesy of *Windsurf Magazine*, by John Severson
p. 138   Courtesy of *Windsurf Magazine*
p. 139   Courtesy of *Windsurf Magazine*, by David Ingalls
p. 140   Courtesy of *Windsurf Magazine*, by Craig Peterson
p. 141   Craig Peterson

Chapter 7

p. 143 left   Courtesy of Windsurf International, Inc.
p. 143 right   Courtesy of Hifly Sailboards
p. 145   Courtesy of *Matt Schweitzer*, by Sylvain Cazenave
p. 147   Courtesy of *Windsurf Magazine*, by Cliff Webb

Chapter 8

p. 172   Phil Berman
p. 173   Phil Berman
p. 173 bottom   Courtesy Tiga Sailboards
p. 174   Phil Berman
p. 175 top   Courtesy Tiga Sailboards
p. 175 bottom   Phil Berman

I. Rigging and Tuning

Even the finest performance equipment money can buy, if not properly rigged and tuned, won't deliver the maximum speed and pleasure it was designed to give. In a sport where equipment is everything, proper rigging and tuning is of the essence.

Choosing the Right Sail for the Conditions

The heavier your body or the lighter the winds, the more sail you're going to need. The lighter your body, or the heavier the winds, the less sail you'll need. The basic goal at all times is to have just enough sail to verge on being overpowered. In other words, if you can't get on a plane and stay there, you need more sail area or more wind, whereas if you get on a plane and can't control the board, you need less sail or wind. If the combination is right, you will get safe, exciting sailing. If you're a beginner, however, there's nothing wrong with going out just a bit underpowered. By taking off the pressure, you can progress at a far faster pace. I recommend a larger board for flotation and a smaller sail for control. There will always be a chance later to go out in a blow and get wild with a higher-powered rig.

To get started, you can use the thirty-five-knot rule of thumb to choose your sail. The general rule is this: as wind velocity increases, sail area decreases, and vice versa, on a one-knot-to-one-square-foot basis:

Wind Speed (knots)	Sail Area
35 K	35 sq. ft.
30 K	40 sq. ft.
25 K	45 sq. ft
20 K	50 sq. ft.
15K	55–60 sq. ft.

Note: More sail is needed for heavier skippers; less sail for lighter ones.

5

Rigging the Sail

Rigging a performance sail is pretty easy, although it's important not to overlook the little things that can cause problems later on. First, lift the mast in the air and let any sand or rocks that may be inside fall out the end. If there's wet sand on the mast or jammed up inside, take it down to the water and rinse it before you put the sail on, since sand in the sail sock will chafe your sail and shorten its life. Worst of all, sand packed between the mast base and the universal can lead to derigging problems, i.e., the mast getting stuck in the universal. If your universal does get stuck so that you and a friend can't get it out of the mast by turning and twisting it, you can always use the "tree method." Start with a five-foot piece of line and tie a hitch knot of some sort around the universal with the other end tied to a tree or some other stationary object, such as the bumper of a car. Then, pull hard on the mast against the universal. After a few good tugs it should come free.

The universal should fit snugly to ensure that the mast won't wobble. This is especially important if you're going to be lengthening the mast by using an extension at the bottom, since any sharp bend near the extension joint will cause a hard spot in the sail and produce an ugly wrinkle coming out of the mast sock. Also, a sloppy universal will make it easier for the mast base to crack or split during a good wipeout. Use tape or plastic, etc., to shim the mast.

The next step is to slide your sail over the mast and put in the battens. With a fully battened sail, you must set the downhaul and outhaul before you can put in the battens. If they are not already in, you can leave them in the sail all the time (unless you prefer to roll up the sail along or around the mast).

At this point, put the universal in the board, tighten the downhaul moderately, and stand the mast up to determine where you want to set the boom and clew. In the beginning, the

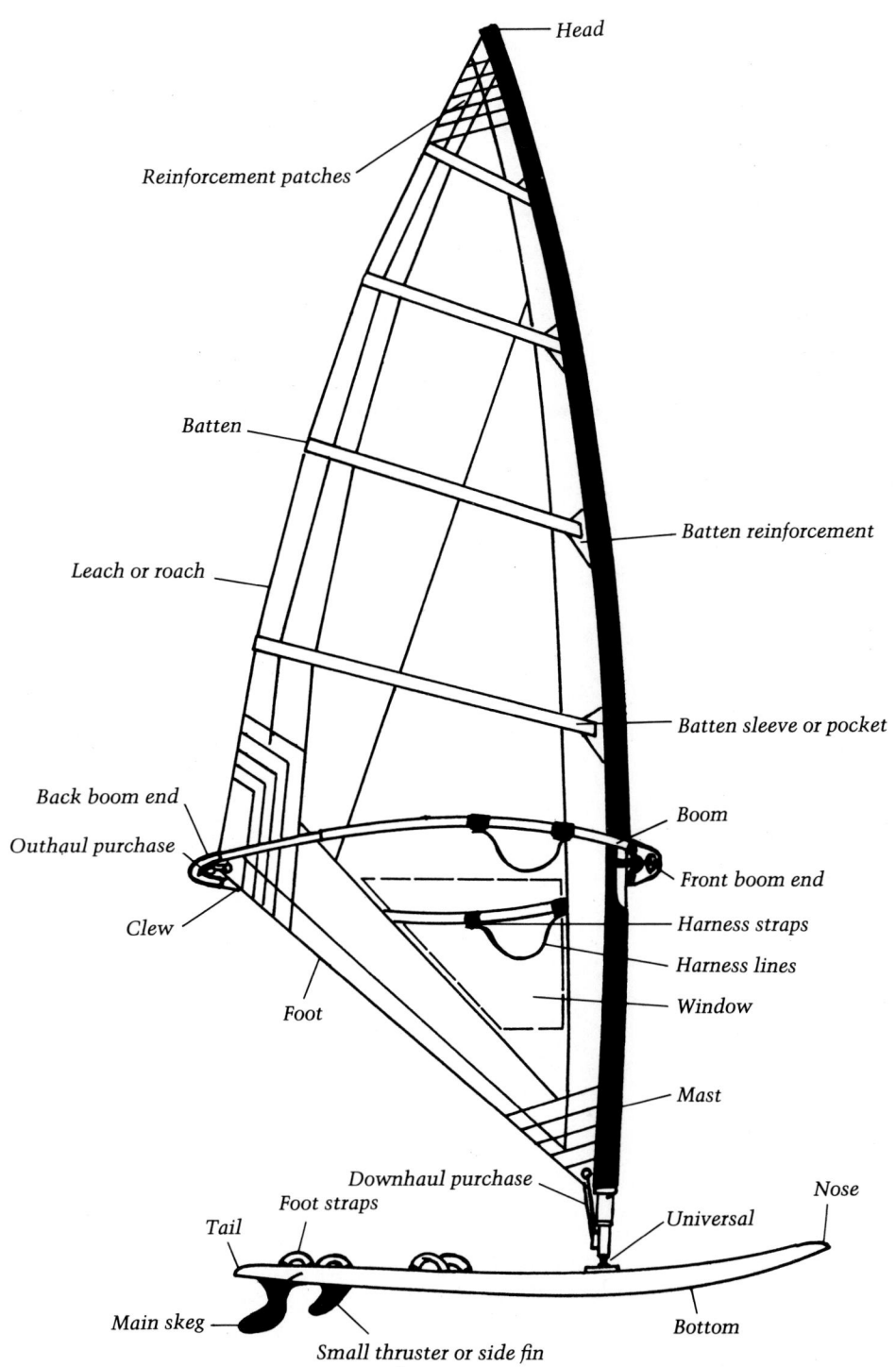

Head

Reinforcement patches

Batten

Batten reinforcement

Leach or roach

Batten sleeve or pocket

Back boom end

Boom

Outhaul purchase

Front boom end

Clew

Harness straps

Harness lines

Foot

Window

Mast

Downhaul purchase

Nose

Foot straps

Tail

Universal

Main skeg

Bottom

Small thruster or side fin

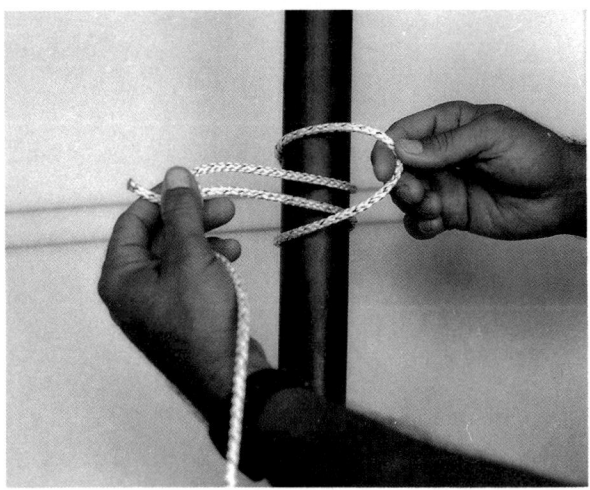

1.1A

1.1B

1.2A

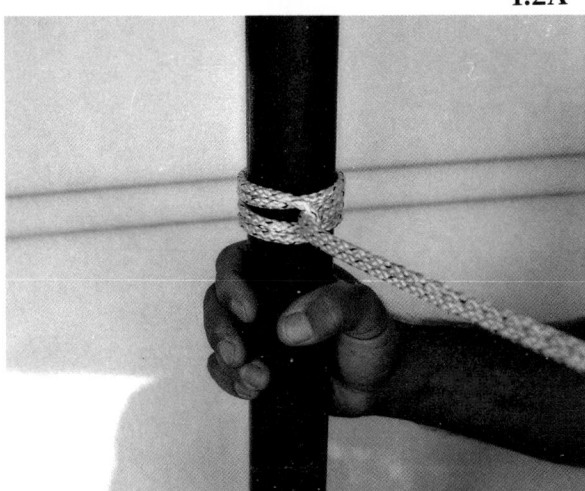

best way to determine proper clew height is to stand on your board with the sail up and look across the boom to make sure that it's very near eye level. If you're looking six inches below it, your clew is too high: if you're looking six inches above it, your clew is too low. Sometimes you can correct such problems by readjusting the boom on the mast, but often the only remedy is either to add an extension to or remove an extension from the top or bottom of the mast.

In actual practice, setting clew height is a matter of personal preference. A number of people set their clews either higher or lower than eye level. I set my own boom at collarbone to chin level, since I feel that a lower boom gives me greater control and comfort. But the eye level guide is a good place to start. After spending some time on the water you can determine what works best for you. Don't be afraid to try several different settings. Be careful, however, to stay within the reinforced area of the mast, especially if you're using adjustable mast extensions.

After deciding on the boom height that suits you, you can save future time by marking your mast with a pen or tape at various points to tell you where the boom should go for different sails and different mast extension arrangements.

Inhaul

Once you've determined the proper boom-height, drop the mast to the ground and slip the boom over it so that it lies nearly parallel to the mast.

Secure the boom by tying the inhaul line to the mast at the preferred height while still leaving enough line free to tie the boom. Then, depending on what type of boom end you have, tie your inhaul line to the boom. Figures 1.1A, 1.1B, 1.2A, 1.2B represent two popular methods of tying off a performance boom end. If you don't see your boom end here, ask your dealer the proper tying technique for your system.

If you are using one or more cleats, remember: never trust it. Which is to say that after you've secured a line to a cleat, it's also a good idea to tie it off around the boom just aft of the cleat (Figure 1.3). This is your best insurance against losing your inhaul or outhaul when out on the water.

Since having the boom set very tightly on the mast is especially important, it's always smart to tie it up when it's set nearly parallel to the mast. Then, when you drop it down to tie it to the clew, you'll stretch the lines, making them tighter, so that they won't stretch any more in the water, assuring a good, tight sail. Be careful, though, when pulling the boom down, not to crack the mast. To avoid this, try using some fairly loose knots until you've gotten a feel for how much they'll tighten up when you drop the boom. If you have to pull on the boom forcefully in order to reach the clew, you can be pretty sure you've tied your knot too tightly and risk a cracked mast if you continue to force the boom any further. Also, before threading the outhaul, make sure the boom end at the inhaul isn't pinching the sail sock since this can cause wrinkles along the foot of the sail.

Since a performance board should always be rigged under tension, it's important that you use line which is both strong and also resistant to stretch. If it's too stretchy, you'll have to come into the beach to retighten your rig. I recommend that you use Marlow prestretch or a similar low-stretch line for your inhaul, outhaul, and downhaul.

Outhaul

Basically, the outhaul controls the amount of draft (curve, fullness) in the entire lower section of your sail. When you tighten the outhaul, you reduce draft, and when you loosen it, you increase draft. The outhaul should be tied according to wind strength. In lighter airs, where more power is needed, you'll want to set the outhaul fairly loosely. This gives a fuller sail, and a fuller sail is a

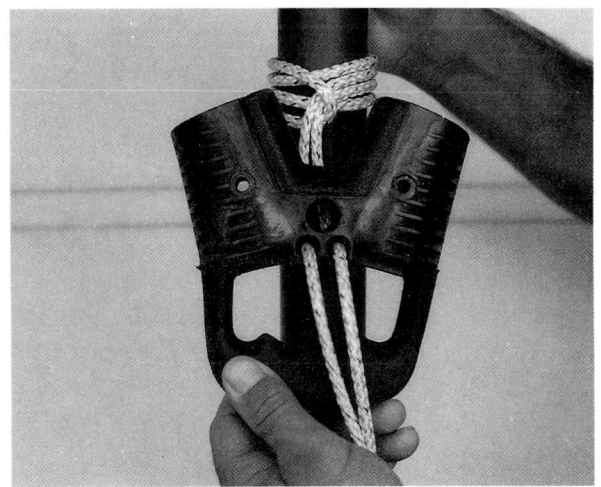

1.2B

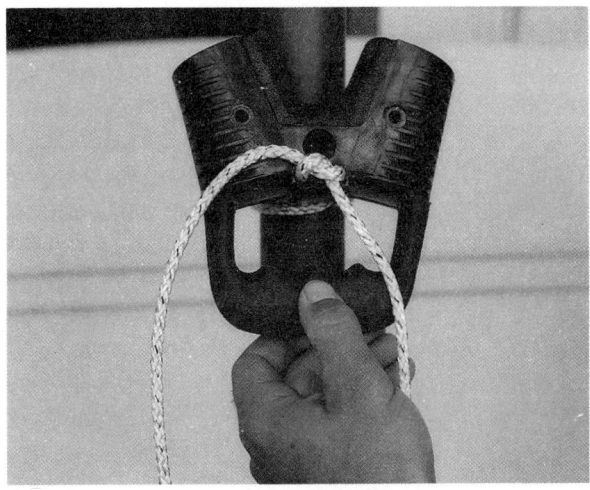

1.2C

1.2D

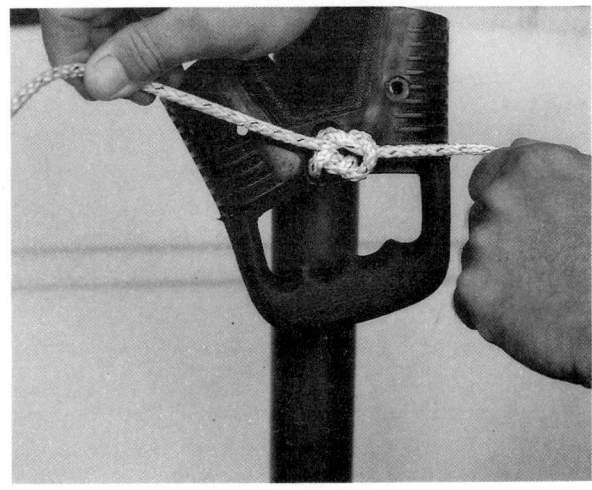

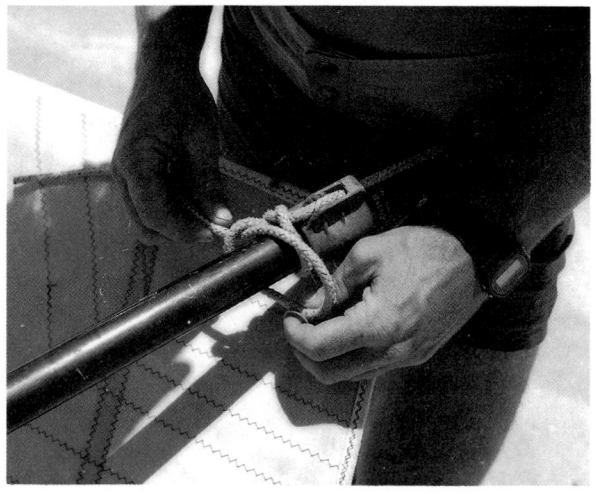

1.3

more powerful sail. In heavier airs, where you may not need or even want additional power, the outhaul should be set very tightly in order to provide a flatter sail shape and shallower draft. This will decrease power. But no matter what type of wind you're sailing in, always go for a smooth sail shape. Never set things so loosely that wrinkles appear, or so tightly that the sail becomes flat like a board.

Like inhauls, there are numerous types of outhauls presently on the market. Again, the chief thing is that your particular system is set up properly. Most importantly, make certain that your lines aren't fouled or crossed if you're using a 3:1 or 4:1 purchase system. Fouled or crossed lines can make it impossible for you to derig unless you cut the line with a knife.

After the lines have been checked, you can tighten the outhaul. How much you tighten it depends a great deal on mast stiffness and sail cut—the stiffer the mast and the less luff curve in your sail, the tighter you need to set it. In most instances, though, performance sails need to have the outhaul set very tightly, regardless of winds or rig setups. To get mine set really tightly, I brace my foot against the boom end while pulling on the outhaul line (Figure 1.4). This provides plenty of leverage. Pull on the outhaul until you remove all wrinkles along the mast and the sail is tuned for the appropriate wind conditions. (Your sailmaker or dealer can be a big help here.) With an RAF-type sail, which I'll discuss in detail later, the sail needs little outhaul tension but a great deal of downhaul tension.

1.4

Downhaul

The downhaul affects the position of your sail's draft (i.e. its point of maximum fullness). The tighter the downhaul, the further forward the draft, or pocket, will move. The looser the downhaul, the further aft the pocket will be. The best place for a performance sail's pocket in high winds is well forward (more on this in Chapter 8). The only exception is in lighter airs, where allowing the draft to remain aft is necessary so that the air blowing over the sail can remain attached to it more easily.

In all conditions other than light air, however, downhaul tension is governed by one principle: you tighten it as much as necessary to keep the draft forward and remove horizontal wrinkles. This is why it's generally accepted that the higher the winds, the tighter you need to set the downhaul. Since winds tend to push the draft aft, more downhaul tension is needed to counteract this pressure and keep the pocket where it should be.

Performance sailing is generally done in medium to heavy winds, so it follows that fairly tight downhaul tension is usually required. To obtain this, most performance sailors rig up a 3:1 or 4:1 downhaul purchase system (Figure 1.5). With such a setup you can put a tremendous amount of tension on the luff. As with the outhaul, it's a good idea to put your foot on the mast base while pulling the downhaul toward your body. This gives you plenty of leverage and holds things in place as you adjust the downhaul to the desired setting. I actually hook the downhaul line into my harness and brace my foot against the universal, using my back to lean into the downhaul to keep the rope from tightening around my hands (Figure 1.6).

One thing that affects downhaul tension is the material of the mast sock. If your sock is made of nylon, for example, you may have to readjust the downhaul after it gets wet since nylon tends to stretch a lot and becomes even more elastic when wet. Dacron, on the other hand, is less stretchy.

However, no matter what sort of material your sock is made of, don't sail with a severely wrinkled luff—adjust it until you obtain a fairly smooth and even sail shape. Here is a

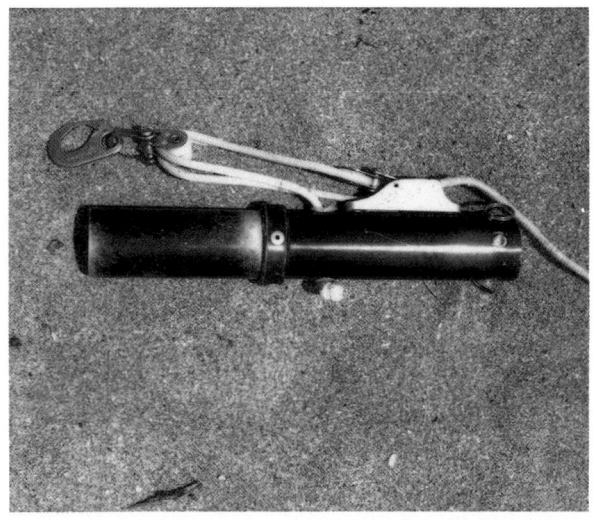

1.5

1.6

basic outhaul and downhaul tuning chart to help you get started:

light wind (15–20 knots)—full foil	medium downhaul light outhaul
moderate wind (20–25 knots)—shallower foil	tight downhaul medium outhaul
heavy wind (25–30 knots)—shallower foil or smaller foil	tight downhaul tight outhaul
gusty wind (varying from moderate to heavy)—flat top, fuller bottom	tight downhaul medium outhaul

Battens

With the outhaul and downhaul tight, you can now insert and/or put pressure on and tune the battens. On non-fully battened sails, you pretty much always stuff the battens in as tight as you can get them. On fully battened sails, this also generally applies, although how tight you tie or Velcro them in can in some instances be determined by wind strength. If you're sailing in relatively light or moderate winds, for example, then tying them in very tightly is often a good idea. This will provide for a fuller sail aloft and give you more power. On the other hand, if it's really blowing, you don't want the sail to be too full up top because this will overpower you. In such conditions, simply stuff the battens in tight enough to remove any creases that form along the batten pockets. This will allow for a freer leech and provide for a faster heavy air sail shape.

As far as the battens themselves are concerned, the best ones are made of Lexan or of glass epoxy, especially if you surf. A Lexan batten can handle some pretty severe wipe-outs without snapping. Fiberglass battens are less flexible and tend to fray or break, but provide slightly better performance, especially if they're made from polyester resins. If you use fiberglass battens, then, tape them on both sides to prevent splintering in the sock and ripping the sail, should they break.

If you have a sail with leech battens, you don't need to worry about how your battens are tapered. But if you own a fully battened sail, the best battens will be tapered, light, and durable. The thin end of the taper always goes in first, toward the luff, with the stiffer, thicker end of the batten at the leech—the trailing edge of the sail.

Harness Lines

After everything else is set up, inspect and attach your harness lines. These should be about three and a half to five feet long, made from stiff rope, and set on the boom with the forward line six to eight inches back from the forward end of the boom and the after line eighteen to thirty inches further back.

Proper adjustment of the harness lines is essential and should be done on the beach before you head out. Lift the sail, hook into your harness, and stand on your board with it pointed so that the wind is on the beam. Properly set harness lines will enable you to sail hooked into the harness with either hand, front or back, dragging in the water or hanging down. In other words, if you can't stay on your feet with just one hand when hooked into the harness, you need to move your lines either forward or aft. If you let go with your front hand and the mast wants to pull away from you downwind, you need to slide your harness lines forward; if you let go with your back hand and your mast wants to fall to windward and the clew away to leeward, you need to move your harness lines back. A perfect balance makes for the most comfortable sailing.

How much loop you should have in the lines is a matter of personal preference. I like to sail with my arms very nearly straight, with

just a slight bend in the elbows. For this reason, I carry a larger loop in my harness lines than those who prefer to sail with their arms more bent. Here, you'll have to experiment to find out which style suits you best. Keep in mind, though, that the straighter your arms, the more you can lean out to windward and gain leverage to fight heel. Speed is maximized if your mast is straight up and down and sailing will be more comfortable.

Another important adjustment concerns the way you tie your harness lines. Here, it's best to use knots that will stay taut under pressure but will allow the line to be loosened and readjusted when slack. A good harness knot lets you move your harness line position while you are on the water without any danger of it coming untied. In Figure 1.7 you'll see the modified figure-eight slip knot system of tying off harness lines. Another way to tie off the harness lines is to loop the lines around themselves and then back up into the pad, as pictured in Figure 1.8. There are also other acceptable ways you'll learn if you ask around.

The board, rider, and sail are an interactive system. Tuning is about balancing out this system so that you get maximum speed from your equipment in any set of conditions. This is why a good sailor is always making adjustments to his equipment and always aware that a little change made in one area may necessitate a change in another area. Since no two boards, sails, sailors, or conditions are identical, it holds that tuning is a highly personal, developmental art.

Tuning

Mast Track Adjustment

Performance boards are quite sensitive to mast position. By moving the mast just a few inches forward or aft in the mast track, you can effect a radical change in your board's feel. Importantly, the mast must be adjusted to balance out the board according to the weight of the rider and the wind, the object being to have fairly equal pressure applied to both the bow and stern. The adjustments needed to achieve this will vary according to the wind conditions and the weight of the sailor. For example, if you're a fairly heavy person sailing in light air and notice that your stern is sinking, making it difficult to plane, you'll need to slide the mast forward in the track until the problem is corrected, or stand more forward on your board, keeping in mind that no matter how you position your mast it's not always possible to stand in your straps (especially if you're not planing). Another rule to go by is that a mast more forward makes a board stiffer in the turns, while a mast set aft makes a board looser in the turns.

Mast Pad

The last thing to do is strap the mast pad around the base of the mast to ensure that your board won't get dinged or chipped when you drop your mast or pick it back up after a fall (Figure 1.9). It seems that whenever I forget this I get a ding in my rail from the universal.

1.9

Rig Check

Just before you head for the water, it's always a good idea to do one last rig check. Look over the entire board and then lift the sail up and sheet it in a bit to check sail shape. If the outhaul or downhaul are not set properly, now's the time to correct things. Also, make sure again that all knots are properly tightened and all cleats tied off. I've broken plenty of equipment on big surf days by making the silly mistake of letting my outhaul come untied at the wrong moments.

Water Check

With the board rigged and tuned, you're now ready to launch and go for a sail (see the next chapter). After you've been on the water for a while, most of your knots, as well as your sail, will have stretched a bit. For this reason, it's often necessary to return to shore after five or ten minutes to readjust the rig—normally, to tighten it. So, if your sail looks wrinkled or the rig feels sloppy, don't hesitate to sail in for a quick readjustment. There's nothing worse than sailing on improperly tuned equipment. Try again! This second tune-up should keep you tuned for the rest of the day.

If the water check indicates that your board is too squirrelly for the conditions (difficult to keep sailing in a straight line), you may want to move your mast forward, move your center fin aft, or install thrusters or larger fins all around. Any one of these measures will make for a stiffer board. On the other hand, if things are too stiff, try taking opposite measures (for more information on these adjustments, see Chapters 7 and 8).

After you've sailed your board long enough, you'll get a pretty good idea of what tuning steps are needed in order to sail your best under any set of conditions. In the beginning, though, you're going to need to do a lot of experimenting. So don't hesitate to return to the beach several times during a day's sail to make different adjustments. Then, go back out on the water and see how they affect your board speed and turning.

Derigging

To eliminate going through all the rigging steps each time you go for a sail, you may prefer just to take out your battens, untie the outhaul, and merely loosen the downhaul, keeping the universal, sail, inhaul, and boom all intack on the mast. Then you simply roll the sail along the leech toward the luff and put the sail into a sail-mast bag and tie off the booms. Now you are ready for an easy, three-minute rig for the next sail. The set back here is that if you need a smaller or larger sail on your next session, you'll need to derig before you rerig.

2. Sailing Your First Performance Board

Part of the thrill of performance sailing in higher winds is that it's a little more challenging than conventional windsurfing. And that's why you must not expect to take to the water and become an instant expert. This is not to say that sailing a performance board is especially difficult, but sailing one well does take practice, a bit of patience, and a spirit of adventure. At first, you'll be falling often as you learn how to turn, uphaul the sail, or do a water start. Since you're unlikely to hurt yourself, the learning process will provide either fun or frustration, depending on how you choose to look at it. My suggestion is to take a playful attitude to it all and let time take care of the rest.

Launching and Beach Starting

Launching a performance board is fairly easy since it's a lot lighter than a standard sailboard. With the board facing the water and the mast to windward, grab the mast with your windward hand below the boom, grab the front footstrap with your leeward hand, lift the board off the ground with your knees, not your back, rest the sail on your head, and carry the entire rig down to the water perpendicular to the wind (Figure 2.1). Then, put the board into the water and wade out as far as is necessary so that you can stand up on the board without hitting the fin on the bottom (Figure 2.2). Now you are ready to beach start. To get going, aim your board on a reach (ninety-degree angle to the wind) and step up on it while sheeting in the sail at the same time (Figure 2.3). If you fall off, no sweat—just start over again.

If you have to carry your board a long way to reach the water, you may find it more comfortable to rest the board on top of your head above the sail (Figure 2.4). Remember, always keep the foot of the sail pointing into the wind when carrying the rig this way.

2.1

2.2

2.3

2.4

Uphauling

If you fall off while sailing a floater or semifloater and are too far from shore to beach start, you may want to get going again by uphauling in the traditional manner used by standard sailboarders. The only difference here is that your board will have less flotation and so will be less stable until you get going. Because of this, you'll have to widen your stance quite a bit in order to keep the board's nose or tail from sinking. The smaller the board, the wider your stance will need to be and the more desirable it will be to perform water starts as opposed to uphauls. However, you won't be able to do a water start if there isn't plenty of wind, and this is why you need to learn how to uphaul the sail if you're sailing on an all-around performance board.

Here are a few tips for uphauling a performance board: First, turn your board so that its sail lies to leeward and you're standing to windward. Now, hop on the board and put one foot in front of the mast and the other foot at least two feet aft of it. (Figure 2.5). If you're sailing on a very short board, your aft foot may need to be as far as four feet behind your front foot to prevent the nose from sinking, since the shorter the board, the closer the mast will

2.5

be positioned to the nose, making it necessary for you to stand further aft to counteract the weight of the rig. Once your stance is set, pick up the uphaul line, crouch down, and pull the sail out of the water by pulling up on the uphaul line and straightening your legs (Figure 2.5A). At this point you may notice the board's nose or tail or one of its sides beginning to sink. If so, then you must adjust your stance until things balance out. In all this, the object is to get the sail up, stop the board sinking as quickly as possible, and get up on a plane.

The smaller the board you're riding, the harder it will be to uphaul since a board with less flotation and a rig set forward needs to be moving before it will stabilize. Standing still in a luffing position is next to impossible on a sinker or semisinker performance board. Consequently, you really can't uphaul one successfully unless you move through the necessary steps very rapidly. You can't hesitate for even a moment between pulling the sail out of the water and sheeting in and taking off. If you do, the board will either sink, flip over, or turn into the wind and stop. Another tip is that when uphauling, the board has a tendency to point into the wind. So get your mast forward immediately as you sheet in to help it bear back off onto a reach.

Once the board is actually under way, you can shorten your stance by one and a half to two feet and should work as quickly as possible to get on a plane (see "Getting up on a Plane" later in this chapter).

2.5A

Water Starting

Water starting really didn't come into vogue until performance boards came on the scene in 1980. I did my first water start by accident while sailing on a Windsurfer in Newport Harbor, California, in 1975. Sailing in a thirty-knot-plus blow, I was knocked down into the water to windward from a gust that came from my lee side, and then picked up again by a gust coming from my windward side just a few seconds later. It was a total accident, since I only lifted the mast to get a breath of air because I was caught under the sail. I didn't realize at all what I had done. I couldn't believe it when it happened and just wrote it off as a fluke maneuver, forgetting about it until we started sailing performance boards on Maui.

2.6

2.6C

Water starting is now considered to be the most effective method to get underway on a performance board, once off the beach. Once you've learned to do it correctly, it requires a minimal amount of effort, and it certainly gets you going again fast. Here is how to do it:

1. In order to initiate a water start, position your mast and board perpendicular to the wind, with the clew of your sail facing downwind and your back to the wind (Figure 2.6).

2. To clear the mast and sail luff of water, grab the mast with your upwind hand anywhere above the boom. Lift the mast as high as you can, swimming a bit to windward, and turn its tip into the wind as the clew of the sail leaves the water (Figure 2.6A). If you're having trouble getting the clew out of the water, swim more to windward as you lift the sail by kicking under water with your feet.

3. Now, your board should still be at a ninety-degree angle to the wind and your mast out of the water and over your head facing into the wind (Figure 2.6B). At this point, place your hands on the boom (Figure 2.6C), trim the sail as you would while sailing (Figure 2.6D), and move the mast forward and/or aft to trim the board (mast forward to bear off, mast aft to head up). Trimming your sail while still in the water helps maintain proper sail shape, and moving the mast

2.6A

2.6B

2.6D

2.6E

forward helps point the board off the wind toward a beam reach, which is the course you'll want for this type of start (Figure 2.6E). The most common error made at this point is not pushing the mast forward enough—this causes the board to turn into the wind. To avoid this, keep the mast forward and the sail trimmed properly, bearing in mind that if the mast is *too* far forward, you'll end up burying the board's nose.

2.6F

2.6G

2.6I

2.6H

2.6J

4. As soon as possible, place your feet on the board to help keep it pointed on a reach (Figure 2.6F). Place your back foot on the board anytime after the mast is out of the water (Figure 2.6B) to help pull the tail to windward. During all of this, try to keep the sail perfectly trimmed.

5. As your board approaches a beam reach, sheet out slightly on the sail by letting off with your back hand. This will help ensure that you aren't sheeting in too much, which would decrease the power needed to pull you up and out of the water. Proper sail trim is essential to pulling your body from the water.

6. Now, pull your body up to your sail while holding it as high and straight as possible to catch the most wind. Also, keep your body close to the board with your knees well bent. This lightens the load your sail has to pull out of the water because it brings your body toward the center of the board, providing for better leverage (Figure 2.6G). In lighter airs, this will really help you in getting up and out of the water (Figure 2.6H). When a gust hits, use the sail to pull yourself up and lean your mast forward just as your body is leaving the water (Figure 2.6I). Now, place your feet in the straps and you'll start to move (Figure 2.6J).

7. The final step is to balance your body, lean back, and begin to plane.

2.7

Remember that a proper water start requires a great deal of practice. Don't be discouraged if it takes time and repetition. To make things easier, there are a few more tips worth keeping in mind. One is that to position your board so that it is perpendicular to the wind, kicking a bit with your feet, is often essential to maneuver into the starting position. (Be careful when kicking like this while sailing over a coral reef, though, since it's pretty easy to kick into the coral and cut up your feet.) Another is that when lifting the sail, the proper body position is to be lying on your back, with the wind at your head and your feet under the sail. If you're experiencing difficulty lifting your mast out of the water, try moving your grip up toward the mast tip. This will also reduce the chances of your clew digging into the water and getting buried.

Whenever you're confused, keep in mind that it's usually easier to move your board into the starting position than to move your sail. This is important to remember when you're in surf and facing an oncoming wave with your mast tip pointing toward shore. If you don't react quickly, your board will be picked up and tossed by the wave, very likely hammering your mast into the sand or reef below. This could easily snap it in two (more on this in Chapter 5). There's one instance, however, when moving the sail is smarter than moving the board—when your clew is facing directly into the wind. Here, you should lift the boom into the air so the wind lifts the clew and flips it over downwind (Figures 2.7 and 2.7A). Then you can turn the board as needed and pick up the mast for a water start.

Initiating a Plane

After you're up and sailing, the first thing you'll want to do is initiate a plane. This is a lot easier to do on a performance board than on a standard sailboard. Gusts are transferred much more quickly to a performance board's stiff and highly tuned equipment, and the board and rig are much lighter.

In light airs or borderline conditions for planing, initiating a plane takes considerable concentration. It is important that the sails be sheeted to perfection and your stance properly balanced to keep the board flat so that you're getting the maximum amount of power from the wind available and the most efficient planing surface possible. As you might expect, this takes practice.

Sail Trim

In the beginning stages, the best way to trim the sail is to use the "conventional" method. This method involves sailing in the direction you want to go, sheeting out until you get a luff, and then trimming in just enough to make the luffing stop. If you don't stop the luffing, you're undersheeted, and if you pull in past the point where the luffing stops, you're oversheeted, or "stalled." This method of checking sail trim can be used on any point of sail.

The problem with the conventional method is that it's slow, and you constantly have to keep an eye on the sail instead of the chop and waves ahead of you. This is why the best way to trim a sailboard sail is entirely by "feel" (i.e. knowing when you've got proper or improper sail trim solely through the use of your hands and arms). If you've no one to race against, the best way to acquire this feel is to practice sailing on a given course for a long

period of time, alternately undersheeting and oversheeting until you get familiar with the way each of these improper sail settings feels. When undersheeting, watch carefully for the first sign of a luff on your sail's leading edge, and when you spot it, note how it affects the feel in your hands and arms. Do the same thing when oversheeting. The most power will be felt with proper trim. Eventually, your sail-trimming motions will become quick and subtle, and this will make you a far faster sailor.

The very best way to learn how to trim your sail properly is to sail with someone faster than you, either when day sailing or racing. By constantly working to keep up with another sailor, you're going to figure out how to trim that sail in no time at all. Pride is a tremendous motivator. It is for this reason that entering one-design or slalom racing contests will help you to progress much faster.

Getting up on a Plane

After your sail is trimmed to perfection, you must prepare to plane (i.e., lift up the board onto a pocket of air so that only its stern is in the water) at the first sign of an approaching gust (Figure 2.8). Just as the gust hits, pull the sail in to obtain proper trim. You can also

pump the sail in and out a few times by letting the rig out slowly with both hands and pulling it back in while the sail remains in the "tuned position" (that is to say, neither luffing nor stalling). Don't change the position of your feet while doing this, but as soon as you start to plane, move your feet further aft. Failure to move your feet aft fast enough may allow your bow to bury, and this will make it either push water and keep you from planing or force it to pearl (dive).

Where you position your feet is entirely dependent upon your board, your body weight, the sea surface, and wind strength. Of these four, wind strength plays the biggest role, since the stronger the wind, the more pressure there will be on your board's sail and nose. In general, the heavier the winds and the rougher the seas, the further aft you'll need to be. In light air, for example, it's not always necessary to get all the way back in the straps. If the nose is lifting too much and pushing water in lighter airs, a better stance is to have your back foot between the aft and forward straps and your front foot between the forward straps and the mast. In most instances, though, especially if you're on a board under nine feet long, as soon as you get on a plane you can get into the forwardmost set of straps.

When winds are strong or gusty and getting on a plane is assured without your having to pump or wait for a gust, it's always smart to move at least one of your feet aft and into the straps before you sheet in and begin to plane. In doing so, there's less danger of your getting launched (catapulted over the bow), and you'll be ready to handle the wind as soon as you sheet in.

In moderate airs, a halfway strategy is appropriate. Here, you sheet the sail in just short of perfect trim, move aft and into the straps, and then trim in all the way and hop onto a plane. Using this method will help you obtain planing speed more quickly and yet avoid the danger of pearling.

In the event that a gust hits you when you're unprepared (i.e. not standing aft enough), release your back hand to sheet out and spill wind and shift your feet aft to avoid a nose dive. When your feet are in the straps, sheet back in and take off.

2.8

Holding a Plane

In strong winds, holding a plane will be the least of your problems. In lighter airs or marginal conditions, however, staying on a plane can require a great deal of work and always demands concentration. Most important in these situations is knowing how to use gusts and where to balance your weight.

In light or moderate airs, using gusts is the key to going fast. When a gust hits, you should immediately trim in the sail and lean farther out in order to hold on to the power you're getting, and you should also try to keep your sail as straight up and down as possible in order to obtain maximum speed. If a gust hits very hard and fast, the draft in your sail will move way aft. To counteract this, you must lean the mast forward as well as lean out with your body in order to avoid rounding into the wind. This will head the board off the wind somewhat and prepare you for a burst of speed. Try to avoid letting a gust hit you unprepared or else you'll either end up getting launched (i.e. thrown over the bow from an out-of-control nose dive), lose the rig to leeward, or head up into the wind.

If winds are really marginal, you may also need to pump the sail frequently to help you hold a plane. This is done, as I mentioned earlier, by slowly letting the rig out with your arms and keeping the sail trimmed and then rapidly pulling it back in in a series of two or three sequences. And as you pump in on the sail, deweight your feet from the board slightly. Each pump gives you the effect of a great and an added burst of speed, which helps hold you on a plane.

Another important technique to master is that of heading up and falling off at the right moments. If you're really slowing and fear that you're about to come off a plane, try heading up into the wind. This will increase apparent wind and help regain attached flow across the leeward side of the sail. After you're back on a plane, you can fall off again to a beam or broad reach.

It's also important to stay light on your feet. If the wind drops, you need to move forward, whereas if a gust hits, you've got to shift aft. How fast or slow you make this sort of move, and how gracefully you make the transitions, will largely determine how long you can stay on a plane and how fast you will go when on one.

Once your board is moving along on a plane, you'll find that maintaining maximum speed on a reach is easy. In fact, it's the same as for any sailboat: you angle higher in the lulls and lower in the puffs to keep a fairly constant speed; you heel the board slightly to leeward in lulls by bending your back ankle to leeward; you ride every possible wave (if you're sailing in swells) by heading off to catch them and heading up when you lose them; and finally, you keep your sail set perfectly by never letting it become over- or undersheeted. Also, if you have an adjustable daggerboard and / or mast track, you'll need to tune it / them properly (see special sections later in this chapter). Another tip is to keep your legs as stiff as possible (not necessarily straight, but rigid), since this translates gusts into board speed far faster than if you let a knee-bend absorb the pressure.

Harness Use

If you plan to use a harness nearly all of the time you're sailing, using it properly is important.

Your harness hook position can be turned up or down. Whichever way you learn is probably how you will stay. I learned with the hook facing down, so that is how I prefer to sail.

Here's how you get in and out of the harness:

Start out sailing on a beam reach and make sure your harness lines are adjusted so you can sail the board with just one hand. You can practice this on the beach. If you can't sail with just one hand (fore or aft), readjust the harness lines until things balance out (see Chapter 1 for more information). Next, hook in as soon as you're on a plane by pulling the boom toward you, allowing the harness line to fall into the hook. Now, start to lean back and rely on the harness line to support your weight in conjunction with the force of the wind pushing your sail to leeward (Figure 2.9). That's it. When you want to unhook, pull the booms toward you, lift or drop your chest, and push away.

After a very short time, getting in and out of the harness will seem as natural as driving a car. However, until you feel very comfortable in the harness, its always smart to unhook from it anytime you feel you are losing control. Taking a fall when hooked in can lead to complications, especially if you let go of the boom. You can become twisted in the harness lines and find yourself trapped under the sail trying to get yourself undone. No fun at all. So, when in doubt, unhook. If you are getting launched and don't have time to unhook, *never* let go of the boom with your hands because you will still get pulled in by your harness. So, keep your hands on the boom and unhook after you've stopped in the water.

2.9

Adjusting Daggerboards

In any breeze over eighteen knots, a daggerboard really isn't necessary unless you want to point higher upwind. And if you have a short, ultra high-performance board, or are riding a slalom board which points very well with its V-shaped hull, you won't even have a daggerboard.

However, if you are sailing with an adjustable daggerboard, the secret to setting it properly is to lower it as far as you can without hydroplaning ("rail-riding," when your board's rail wants to ride to the surface and put your board on "edge") out of control. This means that if you're sheeting out frequently to prevent hydroplaning, your daggerboard is down too far and needs to be raised. On the other hand, if your board doesn't even begin to hydroplane in large gusts, you have it up too far. Ideally, the board will be just on the verge of hydroplaning in heavy gusts. So the secret to setting the daggerboard is to lower it gradually until you achieve this condition. Keep in mind, though, that when sailing offwind, having your daggerboard completely raised is the fastest way to go once you've begun to plane (Figure 2.10).

When heading upwind, the daggerboard normally can be set all the way down because you won't be moving as fast, but "tuning to the point of hydroplaning" just mentioned still applies. In Figure 2.11, for example, this sailor has set her daggerboard in the halfway position to obtain best speed and trim.

2.11

Adjusting Masts

If you're sailing on a larger racing type fun-board which has a mast track that can be adjusted while out on the water (i.e. that can be adjusted with your feet), setting the mast properly is fairly simple. You move the mast aft when you're sailing offwind, as does Ken Winner in Figure 2.12, and you move it forward when you're sailing upwind. Moving it aft offwind helps keep the bow up for high-speed planing and allows you to stand farther aft, which helps reduce the board's wetted surface area. Having it set forward upwind increases the wetted surface area, adding to the board's waterline length, which always benefits upwind performance.

2.12

Turning

The first important thing to know about turning a performance board is that when your daggerboard's not down (or if you don't have a daggerboard), you'll need to rely less on mast angle and more on your feet for turning. This is because you'll usually be turning off a plane with the mast raked well aft, and because the generally downturned rails (refer to Chapter 7 for more information) on this type of board provide most of the bite for turning. You can carve a turn with your feet much faster than you ever could by tilting the mast.

To make a turn into the wind, tilt your aft heel to windward and push away with your foot while simultaneously pulling your front foot slightly to windward (Figure 2.13). To make a turn away from the wind, tilt the ball and toes of your aft foot to leeward, pulling slightly, while simultaneously tilting your front ankle to windward, lifting and pushing your front foot in the same direction (Figure 2.14).

How much pressure you exert with your feet when turning and where you apply it on the board (how close or far away from the rail and tail) will depend entirely upon your speed and just how fast or slow you want to turn. When jibing or tacking, you'll usually need to exert a fair amount of pressure to complete a turn, often by applying a large amount of pressure

2.13

on your whole back leg (see Chapter 3), whereas minor course changes when sailing on one heading won't require much pressure at all. The radical changes you see sailors making on waves is all a matter of pressure on the board and sail trim (see Chapter 6).

Each board reacts a little differently to aft pressure and aft foot position. But no matter what type of board you have, it's important to remember that your aft foot is the main control in turning. The more aft and near the rail you push your back foot and leg, the sharper and faster your turn will be, whereas the more forward and toward the board's center you push your back foot, the more drawn out and slow your turn will be. Another general rule is that the faster you go, the more

your foot needs to be near the rail you're turning on, and the more weight you need to put on that foot, since the faster you go the more you need to sink the rail to execute a turn. The opposite is true when you're moving more slowly.

Another general rule is that the wider your board's tail, the more aft and on the rail your back foot will need to be and the more pressure you'll need to apply to begin and carry out a turn. This is because a wider tail is more difficult to sink than a narrower tail. On a narrower tail, your back foot doesn't have to go way aft. It can remain nearer the board's center, and less pressure will be needed in order to begin and carry out your turn.

Upwind Sailing

For the most part, performance boards aren't made or designed for maximum upwind performance. Since they aren't raced around a course, and since few care to sail upwind for long periods of time unless they are racing, most performance sailors prefer simply to reach back and forth, hop chop and waves, and execute radical turns and jibes. Yet it is necessary to return to your car after a few downwind jibes, so all sailboarders should know how to go upwind, if only for safety's sake.

The first thing to realize is that very short performance boards without daggerboards aren't capable of pointing high into the wind. The reason for this is that unless you sail them fairly far off the wind, you won't get them to plane. And if you don't plane, the board will move so slowly that it'll get blown sideways because it doesn't have a daggerboard to prevent sideslipping. So, the cardinal rule for sailing a short board upwind is that if it's not planing, you're either sailing too high or without enough wind. The only exception would be in a surfing condition, where the speed provided by riding waves generates

enough apparent wind for you to stay on a plane while pointing, even though there is very little true wind blowing.

Naturally, if you're sailing on a longer board with a daggerboard or on a V-hulled slalom board, you'll be able to point considerably higher than you would on a "surfing short board." Also, staying on a full plane won't always be necessary. The daggerboard will prevent you from sideslipping, and you may actually lose ground by falling off too far to get on a plane (i.e. the increased speed you'll get from planing may not always make up for the extra distance you'll have to sail in order to arrive at an upwind destination).

Aside from the fact that nondaggerboard designs need to be sailed upwind at a low angle to the wind, there's very little difference in the way you make one of these or any other sailboard go fast upwind. This holds true for larger performance boards, too. The only significant difference is that you don't trim the sail in anywhere near the centerline of the board. When sailing upwind on shorties without daggerboards, the boom should angle just over the leeward, aft corner of the board. On shorties with daggerboards, you can carry the boom in closer, but never as close to (or past) the center, as you would on a standard sailboard. Carrying the boom in too close when sailing at higher windward angles starves the leeward side of the sail of wind flow, and this puts on the brakes by stalling the sail.

When actually powering upwind, it's still important to lean the board slightly to leeward in order to help the aft rail bite. This is done on a performance board primarily with your back ankle, which should be braced in the footstrap. Using this ankle, you should lean the board to leeward as much as necessary to gain a slight leeward heel. Since my legs are short, I have found that placing the heel of my aft foot near the windward rail and pressing on my footstraps with my toes helps me get extra speed to weather.

To trim the hull in a fore-and-aft fashion, you'll want to try keeping the board on a flat, comfortable plane at all times by adjusting your body weight fore and aft so that the stern is just above the water and the bow is slightly up. If the stern is too low and dragging water, planing will be inhibited. This means you're standing too far aft. If the bow is too low, you'll push water and run the risk of pearling and getting launched. This means you're standing too far forward.

For the most part, wind velocity determines where you need to be—the greater it is, the farther aft you'll need to position yourself to counteract the forward and downward thrust of your sail on the bow. Most properly constructed performance boards will have the straps set so you can deal effectively with a variety of wind velocities. But rarely is it necessary to be in the straps if you're not planing.

Downwind Sailing

Like all sailboats, most performance boards, especially the very short ones, don't sail well directly downwind. It's impossible to generate considerable increases in apparent wind on this heading, and the board has a tendency to submerge and bog down when it's moving slowly. Consequently, most performance sailors prefer to jibe back and forth on broad reaches to arrive at a downwind destination, because doing so is much faster and a lot more fun than sailing directly downwind.

If you must sail downwind, though, the technique for doing so on a larger board is easy. In light air, you stand with your feet parallel, about one and a half feet apart, positioned somewhere near the front footstraps. As winds pick up, you move aft on the board as much as necessary to keep the bow riding just out of the water. You should also try to keep the sail out as far as you can and the board riding level. That's it—until, of course, you begin encountering swells.

On a full sinker or smaller board, it's actually faster to broad reach back and forth to a downwind destination, as we have proved to ourselves in races from Hookipa to Kanala, here on Maui.

Riding Swells

Riding ocean swells or wind waves is one of the great pleasures of performance windsurfing. You can ride them any time you're sailing on a beam reach or lower.

To catch a swell, head your board off as one approaches, tilt the sail forward slightly, and then sheet in. You'll have to lean the mast forward and sheet in hard to counteract the different apparent wind you'll create when dropping down the swell. The greater the wind or swell size, the greater your speed will be and the greater the increase in, and impact of, the apparent wind (for more on apparent wind, see Chapter 8).

As you leave the swell, or get out in front of it, sheet back out by swinging your sail's head to windward and pushing out on the boom, holding a steady course. When the next swell approaches, head up slightly to gain speed, sheet back in again, and start your next descent.

A common problem you may encounter when riding swells is getting blown into the water while trying to accelerate down a wave face. As you lean back to keep your balance while dropping down the swell, you'll naturally begin sheeting in, but you may forget to lean the mast forward as you do so. This weather-vanes the sail, and as a result it comes over on top of you, pushing you in the water. This can be avoided by dropping your body a bit as you descend the wave for added balance, by keeping the mast way forward, and by sheeting in as much as necessary to accommodate any increases in apparent wind. As board speed increases the apparent wind not only increases in strength but also pulls ahead.

Returning to Shore

Always land in a spot where "shore breakers" aren't breaking almost right on the sand. When you find this spot, lift your daggerboard, if you have one, all the way, sail up to the beach, and then slow your board a bit by luffing up or sheeting out. When you're in knee-deep water, hop off the board so your fin doesn't hit the bottom and get torn out of its skeg box—skeg boxes aren't designed to be run aground! Then, pick up your board as you would when launching and carry it up the beach away from the breaking surf. Always lay your sail in a manner so that a gust of wind won't pick it up and hit someone or another board on the beach. That's it.

3. Jibing and Tacking

Jibing a performance board can be a tremendously satisfying personal achievement—not to mention a thrill. In this chapter, I'll introduce you to several styles of performance board jibing, as well as tacking. However, my suggestions here will be of much more use to you after you actually get out on the water and take a few spills. Then, by noting any problems, you can refer back to this chapter to pick up some tips to speed up your progress.

There are many different ways to jibe a performance board, and new styles of jibing pop up regularly. Here are the types of jibes used most commonly today.

Light Air Jibing

When the conditions for your particular board and sail are "marginal," it isn't possible to execute a hard, "carving" type jibe. Under these conditions, if you try to carve too much, the board just sinks and stops. For this reason, jibing on a performance board in light air is very similar to jibing a standard sailboard in the conventional, pivoting method as opposed to the carving style.

To execute a conventional jibe starting from a port tack, do the following:

1. Wait for a good gust of wind and look for the smoothest patch of water you can find.

If chop or small waves are running, try, if at all possible, to jibe when you're well ahead of or between them so that they don't interfere with your turn.

2. To start the jibe, fall off the wind rapidly from a broad reach to a run. This is done by removing your aft foot from its strap and placing it closer to the leeward, downwind rail. The more pressure you put on your back foot, and the farther out on the rail you place it, the faster you'll turn. At the same time, ease out the sail and tilt the mast slightly to the left (to windward).

39

3. As you approach the point where the wind is dead behind you, remove your forward foot from its strap and place it parallel to your aft foot (Figure 3.1). At this time you'll be moving fairly slowly and will need to pivot your board the rest of the way around, especially if the air is light. To do so, put pressure on the port, or outside rail and lean your mast farther to the left, with your sail trimmed for dead downwind sailing (Figure 3.1A). If you need to turn more sharply due to stronger winds, place additional pressure on the windward rail with your windward foot and lean your mast even farther to the left (Figure 3.1B). This will help to guide the board around. However, try to exert relatively equal pressure with both feet in order to keep the board riding as flat as possible. Too much heel will tend to slow you down. Keeping your sail trimmed, your board will come around to the new tack.

4. As the sail reaches the clew first position, let go of the boom with your right hand and let the sail sweep across the bow (Figure 3.1C). As the sail is sweeping across the bow, place your free right hand on the mast (Figure 3.1D) or on the new starboard side of the boom. Now, reach back with your left hand and take hold of the starboard boom and sheet in.

5. At this time, shift your feet from the parallel stance back to the standard sailing stance (Figure 3.1E) and secure them in the straps (if necessary), sheet in, head up a bit, and try to initiate a plane. You may also attempt to switch your feet as the sail is jibing across the bow, but this may confuse you at first.

As you'll learn, executing the conventional jibe on a performance board is not altogether easy. The degree of difficulty depends primarily upon the size of your board and the strength of the wind—the longer the board and the stronger the wind, the easier jibing will be. However, if the wind becomes very strong, then board width also becomes a consideration, since a narrower board can handle high speeds better than a wider board can.

It's important to remember that maintaining maximum speed throughout the jibe is essential. As soon as the board stops, all is lost. For this reason, the sail needs to be let out slowly as you approach dead downwind in order to ensure that it's always drawing at maximum efficiency. You never want to stall to slow down, as you might in heavier wind.

Perhaps the greatest danger to avoid is tilting the board too much with your feet. The way to determine whether or not you're doing this is to check your board speed. If you note that your board slows dramatically while jibing, then you're trying to carve too hard for the amount of wind that's blowing. You need to pivot more and carve less.

Medium Air Jibing

1. To start the jibe, sail along on a beam reach at full speed with your daggerboard (if you have one) fully retracted and your harness unhooked.

2. Now, fall off the wind by removing your aft foot from its strap and applying pressure to the leeward rail by pushing down with the ball of your foot and toes. Leave your forward foot in the strap. At the same time, ease the sail slightly to keep it trimmed to the wind and the new angle of your board (Figure 3.2). Keep your knees slightly bent and apply pressure to your aft leg as you lean it and your body slightly into the turn (Figure 3.2A). Continue leaning with your body, applying constant pressure with your back leg (Figure 3.2B). This first third of your jibe will be the fastest and, due to the increase of apparent wind speed from the turn, it's necessary to sheet the sail in slightly to keep the jibe smooth and flowing (Figures 3.2C–D).

3. As your board passes through the dead downwind position, begin to open up the sail again to get more power and speed (Figures 3.2E–F). Never move your forward foot parallel to your aft foot as you would in a conventional jibe because medium air jibes require that you keep the rail digging in throughout the turn. Moving your forward foot aft would only cause the board to level out, which would make it go straight. Remember, a performance board is controlled more with your feet than with your sail (although sail positioning is also crucial).

4. As soon as you reach the clew first position (Figure 3.2F), let go of the boom with your aft hand, either grab the mast (Figure 3.2G) with your forward hand or slide your hand way forward on the boom of the new tack, let the sail sweep across the bow, and then, as the sail goes across, push the mast forward (Figure 3.2H). While doing all this, don't forget to keep the rail digging in with your back foot (Figure 3.2I). If you don't, the board will straighten out and stop.

5. After you've turned enough to be headed off on a new reach, ease off on the pressure you're exerting with your feet (Figure 3.2J), shift them (Figure 3.2K)—forward foot aft, aft foot forward—and trim in the sail with your back hand to get moving on the new tack (Figure 3.2L).

The most important things to remember about a carving jibe are that you've got to commit yourself to the turn with your feet and you've got to execute it very rapidly. The entire maneuver must be done powerfully, and there can be no delays in the critical transitions—when the sail swings across, your feet must be shifted and the sail retrimmed in an instant.

Two common errors beginners make are not putting enough pressure on their aft foot when going through the turn and letting go of the boom too late. The latter of these problems is the most troublesome, since knowing just when to let the boom go across is especially critical. If you let go too soon, the sail will flip over but the board will still be headed downwind. This will either bring you to a halt or throw you over the nose. If you let go too late, you'll stall the sail and the board will come too far into the wind, throwing you into the water back-first.

It's also important to remember that you want to keep the board on a plane during the entire maneuver. The only way you're really going to be able to do this is to practice jibing until you can move with speed and confidence.

3.2A

3.2B

3.2F

3.2C

3.2D

3.2G

3.2H

3.2I

3.2J

3.2L

3.2K

Finally, keep in mind that it's important not to let your mast go beyond the centerline of the board. You can guard against this by keeping the mast close to your face and chest as you flip the sail around (note Figure 3.2H). In this way, when it flips around to windward, the boom is instantly ready to be trimmed in on the new tack.

Heavy Air Jibing

When it's really howling, jibing a performance board is as thrilling as anything you can imagine. The rush you get from carving a perfect jibe is extraordinary.

Basically, there's little difference between the way you jibe in heavy air and the way you jibe in medium air. In heavy air, you just do everything faster. However, there are a few differences worth mentioning. First, in heavy air jibing, it's easy to lose control due to the high speeds involved. This makes it imperative that you:

1. Jibe in the smoothest patch of water you can find.

2. Exert a large, continuous amount of pressure with your aft foot to keep the inside rail in and biting the water.

3. Oversheet the sail slightly by pulling in on your aft hand in order to stall the sail and bring the leech closer to the eye of the wind, since this will help you maintain control throughout the jibe.

Once you've gotten good at heavy air jibes, you'll find that it's no longer necessary to push the mast forward when coming around. By staying on a plane throughout the turn, that step becomes superfluous. Remember, on a moderate air jibe, you don't let go with your back hand until you are almost all the way around—clew first at least. In heavy air, on the other hand, you don't need to wait until you're clew first; in fact, you can almost release the sail at the dead downwind position. Then, once you've let go, you can hold the mast steady and the board will pivot around it in a clean, full-planing jibe. If your board bounces too much, try moving your aft foot more forward on its rail when you exert pressure.

Here are the steps to completing a high-speed jibe:

1. Begin the jibe as you would a medium air jibe. Take your back foot out of the strap and place it on the rail. But this time, push even harder, really leaning into the turn and setting the board on edge (Figure 3.3) as you begin your turn (Figure 3.3A). If you sense that you are moving too fast and in danger of losing control, ease up on your turning arc and straighten it out a bit (Figures 3.3B–D).

2. When you've regained control and are at a more comfortable speed (Figure 3.3E), start to initiate another turn by putting pressure on your back foot (Figure 3.3F). This is the time to carve hard by leaning way into the turn (Figure 3.3G) and pulling the clew of the sail way in toward your board (Figure 3.3H).

3. To help spill some wind, slightly stall the sail (Figure 3.3I). As soon as you are past the downwind heading, you can begin to open up the sail again to retain speed and get more power in your sail (Figure 3.3J).

4. Earlier than you would in a medium or light air jibe, let go with your clew hand and grab the mast or new side of the boom and let the sail jibe across the nose of your board (Figure 3.3K). Now, sheet in with your new back hand, change your feet (Figure 3.3L), and head up to the desired reach (Figure 3.3M). Hook in, and sail away!

3.3A

3.3B

3.3E

3.3F

3.3C

3.3D

3.3G

3.3H

3.3M

It's important to learn exactly when to let the boom go and how to switch your feet, trim in the sail, and get moving again without losing speed. Naturally, these things are going to take practice. You can expect to wipe out many times at first, but unless you take these practice spills, you'll never enjoy the pleasures of performing one of performance sailing's most thrilling and demanding maneuvers.

After you've mastered the basic jibes, you'll probably want to try a few others. My favorites are the duck, scissor, and one-handed flare jibes.

3.3K **3.3L**

Duck Jibe

The duck jibe is really a variation on the high-speed carving jibe. It's even faster than a carving jibe, though, since the sail draws wind almost throughout the entire jibe. This helps keep the board on a plane and enables you to execute the entire maneuver very quickly without losing speed.

Here are the steps needed to complete a duck jibe:

1. Begin your jibe as you would a moderate air or high wind jibe. Put back foot pressure on the rail (Figure 3.4), carve the turn (Figure 3.4A), and pull the clew in toward the board (Figure 3.4B).

2. Before you near the dead downwind position, prepare to pull the foot of the sail over your head as the leech swings through the eye of the wind (Figure 3.4C). Do this by letting go of the boom with your forward hand (Figure 3.4D) and placing it on the aft section of the boom (Figure 3.4E). Then, let go with your back hand (Figure 3.4F). If you prefer, you can grab the foot of the sail instead of the boom. As you pull the sail over your head with your left hand, try keeping the boom aft. The mast has a nasty habit of wanting to go forward, and you've got to avoid this. If at all possible, keep the mast straight up and in the "sailing position" throughout the jibe.

3. As the rig starts to flip over, duck under the wishbone and grab the front of the boom on the other side with your front hand (Figure 3.4G). At the same time, you can let go with your other hand (Figure 3.4H) and grab the boom on the new tack (Figure 3.4I).

4. During the entire maneuver, keep the board carving with your feet toward the new tack, applying constant pressure on the rail with your back foot (Figure 3.4J). Keep the sail's clew open (Figure 3.4K–L), switch your feet (Figures 3.4M–N), and then continue heading up toward the new reach (Figures 3.4O–P).

5. After the jibe is completed, stop carving with your feet and trim in the sail to gain full speed on the new tack (Figures 3.4Q–R).

3.4A

3.4B

3.4E

3.4F

3.4C

3.4D

3.4G

3.4H

3.4I

3.4J

3.4M

3.4N

3.4K

3.4L

3.4O

3.4P

It's important to remember that duck jibing is a full carving, planing maneuver. You must have good speed throughout the turn in order to complete the jibe successfully. The big trick is knowing when to pull the sail through the eye of the wind. If you pull it across too soon, you'll end up with your sail clew first and your board still on the original tack. On the other hand, if you pull it across too late, you'll lose downwind speed, and as the sail comes through the eye of the wind it will get knocked down into the water. The key here is board speed, so that as you pull the sail across, the wind's affect upon it is minimized by the fact that your board is traveling nearly or just as fast as the wind is blowing. Also, avoid oversheeting on the new tack. It's usually necessary to sheet out quite a bit on the new tack to gain proper trim (note Figures 3.4L–M).

3.4R

Scissor Jibe

The scissor jibe is the tightest possible jibe you can make on a performance windsurfer. It's the perfect jibe to use whenever you're in a tight spot and need to change direction quickly.

Here are the steps needed to perform a scissor jibe:

1. To start the jibe, fall off slightly from a beam reach toward a broad reach (Figure 3.5), although you can also perform this jibe while remaining on a beam reach.

2. When you're ready to initiate the jibe, place both feet on, and apply pressure to, the extreme aft portion of the board's tail, putting most of the pressure on with your inside leg (Figure 3.5A). As you turn, pull the sail way over on top of you to slow down (if you really need to slow down, as you might in heavy air, drop your butt off the tail and drag it in the water a bit) (Figure 3.5B). At the same time, push down hard with your feet to raise the nose of the board. This is the trickiest part of the jibe, since you actually "pop a wheelie" in order to spin the board around in a tight arc off the tail. You don't carve as much as pivot on the tail as it remains stationary in the water.

3. After you've slowed down enough, lean the mast forward and to the side (Figure 3.5C), as in a conventional jibe, and pivot the board with your feet, still pushing hard with both legs (Figure 3.5D), but hardest with your inside leg. You push down with both legs to lift the nose and sink the tail, and you push a little harder with your inside leg to execute the pivot.

4. As the board passes through the downwind position (Figure 3.5E), begin to open up the sail and straighten your legs and the mast (Figure 3.5F).

5. When the boom reaches the clew first position and the board is past halfway around (Figure 3.5G), let go of the boom with your aft hand (Figure 3.5H), grab the mast with your forward hand (Figure 3.5I), pull it forward (Figure 3.5J), and then let the sail sweep across the bow to the other side as the board is completing its spin. Doing all this during the spin is important because the board will pivot very fast, and you don't want to end up pointing directly into the wind before your sail comes around.

6. Just before releasing the boom, shift your feet to prepare for the new tack (Figure 3.5J). Then, as soon as you can, grab the boom (Figure 3.5K), sheet in (Figure 3.5L), and get ready to plane.

3.5A

3.5B

3.5E

3.5F

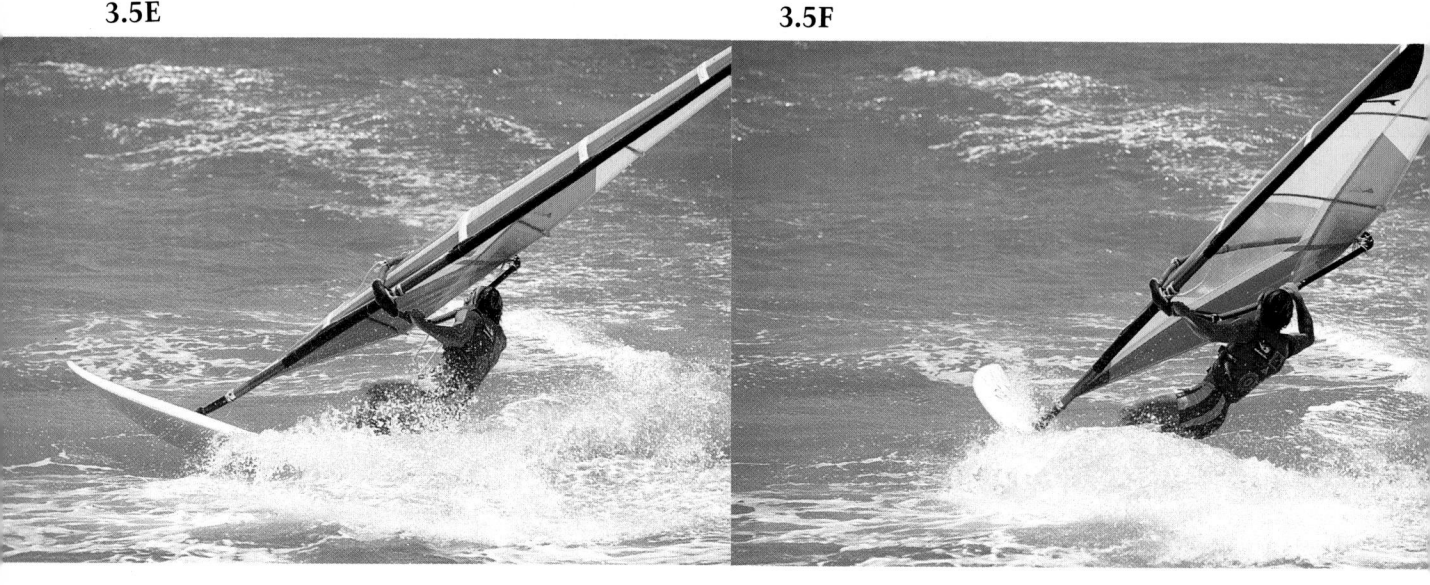

3.5C

3.5D

3.5G

3.5H

3.5I

3.5J

3.5K

3.5L

The scissor jibe isn't an easy one to get the hang of. It's going to take you some time to figure out how much you'll need to slow down, how high the bow will need to be lifted, and how you can pivot the board around in such a tight radius using only your feet. After you get it wired, though, you'll find that you can successfully perform scissor jibes with far greater consistency than almost any other jibe.

Possibly the most important part of doing a scissor jibe well is knowing how much to stall. The stronger the wind, the more you must pull the sail over your head and the greater the wheelie you must pop in order to slow the board down so you can execute your pivot (Figure 3.6).

3.6

One-Handed Flare Jibe

In addition to the duck and scissor jibes, you may also want to do one-handed jibes. In these jibes, everything is done exactly as if you were executing a high-speed jibe except that you let go with your aft hand during the turn and drag it in the water, letting your feet alone pull you through the turn. Dragging your hand in the water does absolutely nothing—it's just a flashy way of showing how well you've got things wired. What this jibe really does is allow you the chance to be playful and get a little cocky, which is fine as long as your hand is the only part of you that ends up in the water!

A few of my favorite jibes are the one-handed duck jibe performed by Matt Schweitzer (Figure 3.7), the one-handed flare jibe performed by Pete Cabrina (Figures 3.8A–C), and the pirouette jibe shown here of yours truly and photographed by Steve Wilkings (Figures 3.9–9K).

3.8

3.8A

3.8B

3.8C

3.9

3.9A

3.9B

3.9E

3.9D

3.9C

3.9F

3.9G

3.9H

3.9K

3.9J

3.9I

Tacking

Performance boards, especially the very small ones, are notorious for tacking poorly. Yet, while it's true they're somewhat difficult to tack, they're not nearly as tough as popular opinion would have you believe. The real reason why people think they tack so poorly is that most sailors prefer to jibe when changing tacks. In other words, since few people actually practice tacking performance boards, few can tack them well.

Size and buoyancy are what determine how hard it is to tack a board. The smaller the board, for example, the more difficult it will be to tack. Since smaller boards lack stability, have a tendency to sink when they're not moving, and have their masts positioned very close to their noses, the only way you can tack one successfully is to keep it moving fast. Larger semifloaters, on the other hand, can be tacked pretty easily. When riding one of these, the procedure for tacking is nearly identical to that used for tacking a standard sailboard.

To tack a short board, it is important to keep a few extra tips in mind:

1. To initiate the tack, lean the mast back while pushing with your back aft foot and pulling with your forward foot (Figure 3.10). Now, place your hand on the boom or mast (Figure 3.10A), move your forward foot just in front of the mast (Figure 3.10B), and keep your aft foot between your forward and aft footstraps. Be sure to keep pushing with your aft foot in order to keep the nose from sinking.

2. As soon as your board comes into the wind, it will slow down due to a lack of momentum. Now you must pull the boom over the back of the board until it crosses the centerline (Figure 3.10C), lean the mast aft, and then jump over to the other side of the board, letting go with your back hand (Figure 3.10D).

3. As soon as you're on the other side of the board, push the mast forward to bear off more, push down hard with your aft foot to keep the nose from sinking, and sheet in and try to get moving as fast as you can to regain stability (Figure 3.10E). Then, step back into the straps and begin to plane on the new tack (Figure 3.10F).

At first, chances are you won't get around the mast fast enough and the nose will sink. If this happens, it's essential that you take a very wide stance as soon as you cross the board. By positioning your back foot way aft, you'll counterbalance the nose sinking and enable yourself to maintain stability until you can sheet in and get moving.

3.10

3.10C

3.10B

3.10A

3.10D

3.10F

Another important technique for maintaining stability during the tack is to try keeping your body as close as possible to the centerline of the board. This increases lateral stability, and as a result, it'll help you keep your board up.

Now that you know the basic steps of jibing and tacking your performance board, it's time for you to get out on the water and carve a few turns. By practicing and reviewing this chapter from time to time, you're bound to get it mastered. Have fun!

4. Chop Jumping

Whether they sail on lakes, rivers, or oceans, the great majority of performance sailors do most of their jumping off chop. Basically, there are four parts to jumping: approach, takeoff, aerial trim, and landing. To be a good chop jumper, you need to master each part.

The Dynamics of Chop Jumping

The type of jump you do off chop is mainly determined by how much board speed you have and the shape of the chop you're jumping. Board speed determines how much time you can spend in the air, and chop steepness determines whether you can go for a high jump or a long, low jump. The steeper the chop, the higher you can go. The more gradual the incline of the chop, the farther you can jump.

In practice, you really won't be able to determine the type of chop jump you're going to make until just prior to or shortly after takeoff. While you're learning, be sure to jump every substantial piece of chop that comes your way; don't limit yourself to performing only one type of jump. If the board speed's there and chop pops up, go for it!

Note: The types of jumps and landings discussed in this chapter also apply to wave jumping, covered in more detail in the next chapter.

Approach

The approach to any jump is critical. A good approach will enable you to hit the chop at full speed, just as it's about to break. If you arrive either too early or too late, you'll lose the steepness necessary for a vertical takeoff. That's why learning to read the chop so that you can time your approach just right is an important part of jumping.

The only way to ensure that you'll be moving at full speed just prior to the jump is to be on a beam reach. In most instances, though, this will put your board nearly broadside to the chop. So, what you'll have to do is find which tack will head you most into the chop while still beam reaching (Figures 4.1–4.1A). This is the tack on which you'll be able to jump the highest because you won't have to head up as much in order to point the board into the oncoming chop.

Once you're sailing along on the correct tack at full speed, the next step is to pick out the piece of chop you want to jump. The best piece will be the biggest and steepest one you can find. If possible, try to time things so you'll hit it during a gust or puff. This is the ideal situation for jumping—maximum wind and board speed combined with the steepest possible ramp.

4.1

Takeoff

When you see a good piece of chop coming, head up from a beam reach toward a close reach at the last possible second so that you're heading more into the oncoming chop and yet still moving at maximum speed. What you want here is to point only your board higher into the wind and chop, keeping your sail trimmed for a beam reach in order to maintain your speed.

As you begin climbing the chop, keep your knees rigid but slightly bent, as you do while sailing, and trim your sail in tight, setting it for a broad reach. After the board's nose is well out of the water and angled skyward, push down and sideways on the fin with your aft foot just as the tail is about to leave the water. Then, tilt the board slightly to leeward with your ankles and lift slightly on the boom while squeezing in the sail. The springing action caused by applying pressure to the fin combined with leeward ankle pressure will help to unweight the board and raise the windward rail slightly. At this time, suck your legs up toward your chest to help the board out of the water. Having the rail raised is essential; it forces the wind to blow under the board, which helps keep it in the air, and it blows the bow to leeward, so that you land on a beam reach rather than on a close reach.

Remember, the only time you want to be on a close reach is just prior to takeoff. Once in the air, you must immediately return to a beam reach. This is the only heading that will allow you to get a good amount of height or distance into your jump and still maintain a "reasonable degree of control." I'll let you define that!

Another important tip to keep in mind is that you should lean out as you're leaving the water. This is essential for a good jump. Don't ever be afraid to squeeze in the sail and really lean your weight into it.

Aerial Trim

Once you're in the air, you must keep the rig leaned over to windward during the entire jump. It will then act as a kite to help keep you airborne. If you don't, you'll lose power and drop. Also, try to keep the bow of the board from getting too close to the wind. If this occurs, either push away with your forward foot and pull in with your aft foot or tilt the mast forward a bit. If things get really bad, you may have to do both things at once. Another trick is to try lifting the windward rail—this helps keep the nose from pointing into the wind because it allows the wind to push the nose down, directing it more toward a beam reach.

Although not as critical, it's also important not to let the nose of the board blow too far downwind. To keep this from happening, don't tilt the board so much to leeward but keep it flatter. In very strong winds this is necessary because facing the bottom of the board into the wind causes the nose to blow downwind, landing you on a broad reach.

Long Jump

If you want to go for a long horizontal jump, you'll have to level out your board as you leave the water (Figure 4.2). In most instances, this means lifting up its tail with your aft foot as soon as you become airborne. How much you'll need to lift will depend upon your speed as well as the angle of your takeoff. In general, as soon as your nose and tail are horizontal, you can stop lifting. Once the board is riding relatively level, you should keep it in trim primarily with sail adjustments. If the nose gets too high, sheeting in a bit will force it back down.

4.2

High Jump

If steep chop is present, you may want to go for a high jump—the steeper and higher the chop, the higher you'll be able to fly (Figure 4.3). To do so, never lift the stern until you're as high as you can possibly go, and always aim your board toward the sky when taking off. However, never try going straight up—you'll only come straight back down! In other words, a certain amount of forward momentum is necessary in order to make a good landing.

4.3

Landing

Eventually, the man who goes up must come down. Basically, there are four ways of doing this: tail first, nose first, "horizontal tilt," and flat. Landing flat can be eliminated right off the bat—it breaks boards and can cause ankle, foot, and knee injuries.

Tail First

The tail-first landing is the easiest and safest way to land (Figure 4.4). By having the tail hit the water first, there's little danger of pearling or getting tossed over the bow. If you keep your board and sail trimmed properly on takeoff, you'll have set yourself up well for a tail-first landing. To land in this manner, lift with your forward foot and push down with your aft foot while sheeting out the sail as much as necessary to keep the nose from hitting the water first. Ideally, the nose will touch down right after the tail. This keeps the board from "putting on the brakes" when you land and allows you to pick up speed in preparation for your next jump.

As you touch down, your legs and body are going to be jarred by the impact. This can be dealt with by bending your knees as much as necessary to counteract the jarring. In other words, let your legs act as shock absorbers. The higher the jump, the more you'll need to bend your knees.

4.4

Nose First

A faster but more dangerous landing is the nose-first approach (Figures 4.5–5A). The danger, of course, is that you'll stick the nose in too far and get catapulted over the bow by the sail, which generally isn't too much fun. There's an advantage to landing nose first, however. If you do it right, the board will land on a plane without pushing any water, which is ideal for surf slalom racing or just keeping your speed up for the next jump.

To land nose first, push down with your forward foot and lift up with your aft foot while sheeting in the sail as much as necessary to put the nose in the water just ahead of the stern. Remember, a performance board's nose has a good deal of kick. This means that you can angle the board down without the nose immediately submerging. It's also important to keep your weight way back on the board by extending your arms and legs forward. This enables you to keep the nose up sufficiently and still maintain proper sail trim. The board and sail really don't move—only your body moves, aft, actually hanging off the back of the board. This permits the board to level off as soon as it lands.

4.5A

4.5

The Ideal Landing

For all conditions, the ideal way to hit the water is to land the nose section of your leeward rail slightly tipped to leeward. By tipping the rail, you keep the board from slapping flat against the water and enable it to glide almost instantly onto a new plane. To land in this fashion, simply adjust your feet and sail so that your board's ready to touch down on a horizontal plane and then, just before it hits the water, tilt it slightly to leeward by pushing down with your toes.

On higher jumps, where more often than not you'll have to land nose first, leveling out can be pretty difficult. Here, the best thing to do is keep your weight way aft in order to prevent a pearl (Figure 4.6). On longer jumps, your landings will be faster and smoother, and you'll often be able to land right on a plane.

Given the variety of landing styles just mentioned, the potential for goofs abounds. So don't be bashful about bailing out anytime you think your board is out of control. Even the most expert jumpers can't avoid making mistakes. And the smart ones, the ones you see sailing all the time because they aren't laid up with an injury, are never afraid to push the rig away and take a dive. So use caution and never, never be afraid to bail out if she's burning up on reentry—push the eject button and pop the chute to windward!

4.6

5. Wave Jumping

Wave jumping is actually easier than chop jumping because waves are more consistent in size and shape. With waves, you have a lot more time to plan your approach; you don't have to search for a jumpable wave as you do a jumpable piece of chop. Once you've learned to handle chop, don't waste any time trying your hand at waves, since doing so can radi-

cally improve your jumping skills. First, though, you'll need to learn a little about how waves form and break. And you'll need to consider different wind types and how they affect jumping. Then you can take the information from the last chapter and apply it to takeoffs and landings according to wind directions.

Anatomy of a Wave

Most waves that break near shore have a peak and a shoulder (Figure 5.1). The peak is the highest point of the wave, much like the peak of a mountain. The shoulder is the part of a wave that gradually slopes down from the peak until it reaches the trough. A wave can have either one or two shoulders. The object

in wave riding is to follow one of these shoulders for as long as you can.

Waves also have lips, bottoms, and faces (Figure 5.1A). The lip of the wave is the edge of water near the peak that curls over and breaks down the shoulder. The spot where the lip has just broken is where the wave is most

5.1

PEAK

RIGHT SHOULDER

LEFT SHOULDER

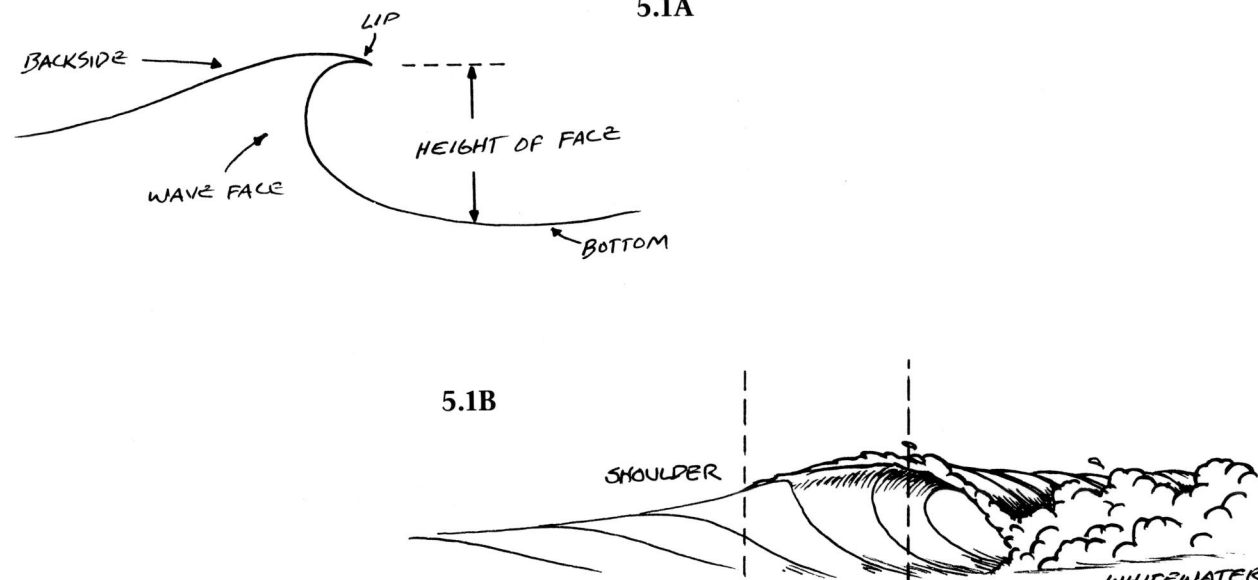

5.1A

BACKSIDE

LIP

HEIGHT OF FACE

WAVE FACE

BOTTOM

5.1B

SHOULDER

BOTTOM

WHITEWATER

CRITICAL SECTION

powerful. This is called the critical section of the wave (Figure 5.1B). The bottom of the wave is the point where the face (i.e. the vertical front) of the wave levels out from a vertical plane to a horizontal plane.

As you might guess, peaky waves, or peaks, have both lefts and rights. Waves that break in one direction (i.e. that have one shoulder) are called either "lefts" or "rights." If the shoulder peals off to the left (when facing shore from the surfline), then it's a left, and if it peels off to the right, then it's a right. (Figure 5.1B shows a right.) Waves that break in both directions have two shoulders and are called "peaky." (Figure 5.1 shows a peaky wave with both a right and a left.)

Out at sea, waves don't break unless they're very large because a wave normally won't break until it reaches a bottom depth equal to half its height. In other words, a six-foot wave will break in about three feet of water. How soon a wave breaks (wave speed) and how much force it breaks with (wave power) are dependent upon offshore bottom contour (i.e. the contour of the bottom near shore). If the

bottom near shore slopes very gradually out to sea, as it does on most of the eastern coast of the United States, incoming waves will be slowed by friction as they move toward shore. Such slowing makes for waves that crumble and are weak in relation to their size. They have minimal concavity to their faces, well-defined peaks, and slow-moving shoulders with hardly any lip. Called "mushy," these waves are perfect for beginning surfers because they move so slowly that the danger of pearling at the bottom of them is much less than with faster, stronger waves (Figure 5.2).

Mushy waves are also good for beginning jumpers. They're not so steep that there's

MUSHY WAVE

5.2

danger of getting caught by a hard-breaking lip, and because they're less powerful, there's also less danger of hurting yourself or your equipment should you wipe out in the lineup.

At the opposite end of the spectrum are hollow waves, or "tubes," the kind of waves you commonly find on tropical islands, or at steep and shallow beach breaks (Figure 5.2A). These waves break very fast because they reach shore from extremely deep water. Here, the bottom near shore drops off sharply rather than sloping gradually out to sea. As a result, these waves encounter very little bottom resistance until they're just about to break and so aren't slowed down as mushy waves are. When they do break, their faces are very steep and their lips peel over with tremendous speed and power. Only fairly advanced surfers should take on good-sized hollow waves. If you get stuck in the lineup after a bad wipeout, you're likely to get pounded unless you can instantly pull off a water start and get moving.

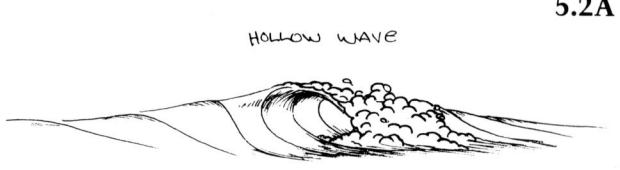

5.2A

HOLLOW WAVE

Another type of wave is a "closeout" (Figure 5.2B). These are waves that have poorly defined peaks and unevenly breaking shoulders. They can be jumped but are not ideal for surfing because you can't follow their shoulders toward shore. All you can really do is get one good turn and then ride them straight in.

5.2B

CLOSE-OUT WAVE

Wind Types

Just as important as knowing wave types is knowing wind types. Basically, there are five types of winds to watch for: onshore, offshore, sideshore, sideonshore, and sideoffshore (Figure 5.3).

For a lot of sailors, an onshore wind is the only thing that makes waves. Although a little more difficult, this direction makes for good and fun conditions for jumping. To get out through the surf, you must sail at an angle that puts your board nearly broadside to the waves, which makes things pretty tricky. In fact, if the waves are too big or the wind is too light, getting out can be impossible because the only way to hit a large breaking wave is to meet it head on. To hit a wave head on in onshore conditions, you've got to turn nearly dead into the wind, which brings you to a halt at the worst possible time. Onshore

conditions can be a lot of fun, however, as long as the waves aren't too big or the winds too strong. (See Jumping on Sideonshore for techniques to get out.)

Straight offshore winds are difficult to jump or surf in if the waves are of any considerable size. Like onshore winds they'll cause you to lose power when you're trying to get out; but where onshore winds do this by making you sail too far into the wind, offshore winds do it by making you sail too far off the wind. The greatest danger with jumping in offshore winds is getting caught up in uncontrollable winds that will literally blow you away in midair. It's very gnarly and highly inadvisable to attempt riding or jumping waves in straight offshore conditions. Only when the wind

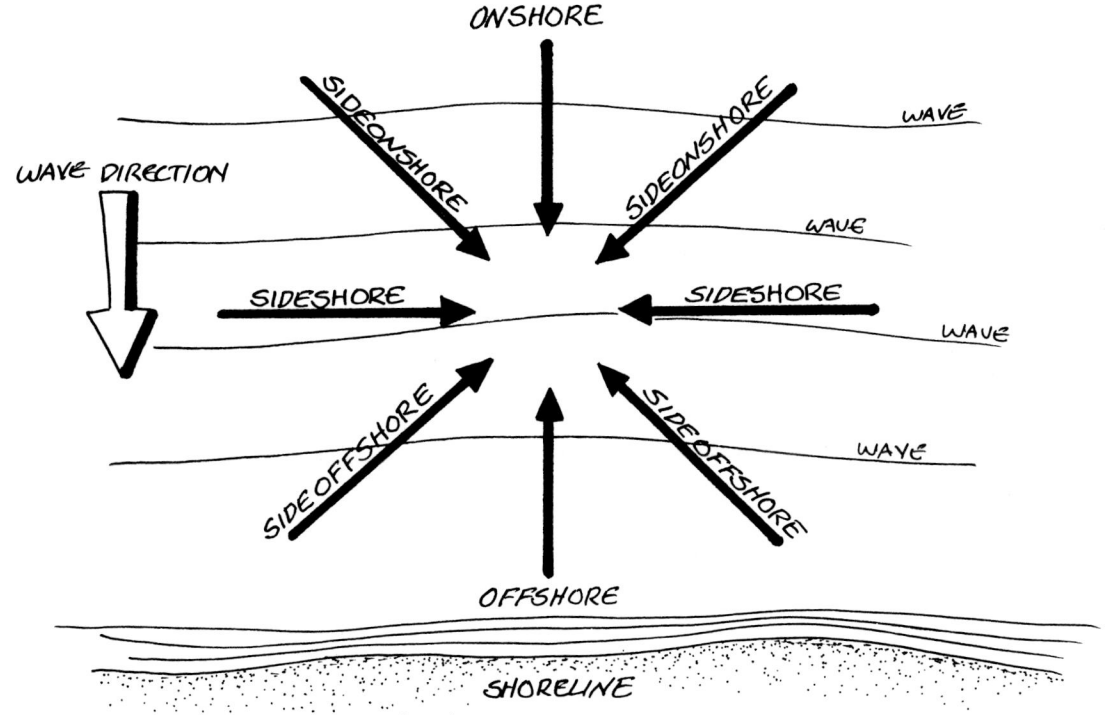

swings to one side or the other of directly off-shore should you consider conditions suitable for sailing in the surf.

For these reasons the ideal wind direction for jumping and surf riding is sideshore or something very close to it. With a sideshore wind, you can punch out through the surf on a full-speed beam reach and then ride the waves back in at full speed, going either right or left, close-hauled or beam reaching. Unfortunately, the winds won't always be blowing directly sideshore. In fact, the two ways it usually blows are sideonshore and sideoffshore. Each of these winds requires its own particular jumping and surfing technique. In the following sections, I'll discuss how all three of these wind types affect wave jumping. Then, in Chapter 6, I'll discuss how they affect riding back in through the surf.

The type of jump you do is mainly dependent upon how and when you approach and take off on a wave. Since a beam reach is the only way to fly and land, I'll talk more about technique in the following section on jumping in sideshore winds. This doesn't mean, though, that what I have to say about jumping in this wind type doesn't apply to all wind types. The important thing is that you take the precautions I'm going to suggest for dealing with less than ideal winds and then alter your style accordingly so that you can jump in them both safely and effectively.

In most instances, if you have good wind and board speed, you can perform a wide variety of jumps. In light winds, though, where board speed is limited, you'll want to avoid hitting waves that are just about to break or that have just broken; otherwise, you'll find it very tough getting out. And this can be true in heavy airs, too, as Dave Ezzy knows from experience at Hookipa! (Figures 5.4–4B). In light airs (and sometimes also in heavy airs) you'll often need to sail way out on the shoulder in order to avoid heavy foam (treated in detail shortly), and you'll have to be careful about directly approaching a steeply breaking lip. Remember that unlike chop, which pops up intermittently, waves keep on coming in. Normally, they arrive in sets of three to five big ones and then four to ten smaller ones. The big sets usually occur regularly and can be timed. If you want to avoid big waves when heading out, count how many waves are in the sets and determine the interval of time between sets. But no matter how good you are at timing the waves, do keep in mind that mother nature can and does like to play tricks. In other words, a huge cruncher is always lurking just over the horizon!

5.4

5.4B

5.4A

Launching in Surf

After you've got the surf conditions wired, you can launch your board and power out through the lineup to "get air" off a wave. When you're launching in the surf, the preferred method is the beach start (see Chapter 2). If you study the waves carefully, you should be able to time your start during a lull. And if you can spot a channel or an area where the shorebreak is smaller, you'll probably want to start there.

Getting out Over White Water

Once you're up and moving, the object is to power out through the lineup so you can make a jump or turn around and surf a wave back in. How you do this will depend largely on the way the waves are breaking and whether or not you want to do some serious jumping.

But whether or not you want to jump, first you've got to get out through the shorebreak and the foamline. Hitting foam is a lot different from hitting an unbroken wave.

Whenever you hit a piece of foam, your board will slow. How much it slows will depend on how much wind and speed you've got and how much foam you are hitting. The more wind, the more foam you can deal with and still maintain full speed.

In sideshore winds, foam can be handled pretty easily. The object here is to sail as fast as you can and then lift the nose over the foam at the last possible second, sort of like "popping a wheelie" over a curb on a bicycle. This allows the foam to flow under the board and enables you to climb over it. After the foam has passed, you may want to bear away a bit to build speed again.

When a wave breaks in front of you and churns up a lot of white water, try to avoid the spot where it has just broken—the spot where the white water has the greatest power because it has had less time to dissipate (Figure 5.5). Ideally, you'll bear away or head up to go around heavy foam—sometimes you may even want to jibe to avoid it! Any method is fine, as long as you turn directly into the foam when it's no longer possible to turn back or sail around it.

In sideonshore winds, when you've got to power out at an angle, you should head up and jump the foam only at the last possible second. Then, as soon as your board is over it, it's essential that you push the mast forward and turn the board downwind in order to regain speed on a beam reach.

In sideoffshore winds, you've also got to power out at an angle. Here, however, you should fall off at the last possible second and hit the foam head on. As soon as you've begun climbing the foam, head back up to regain speed. Be prepared for wind turbulence, though, since the foam will be between you and the wind. And remember, always climb over breaking waves straight on. But swells can be jumped at an angle.

Once you've got past the worst part of the foamline, and it's possible to ride over shoulders or hit waves close to the lip for a jump, deciding what to do is up to you. If the waves are breaking far apart or you're approaching the last one in a set, you may want to go for a high jump. If a big wave is coming after the one you're jumping, though, be careful. If you land too late or wipe out, that outside wave will catch you when you're down. This is the time to go for a long jump and maintain speed, as does Pete Cabrina in Figure 5.6.

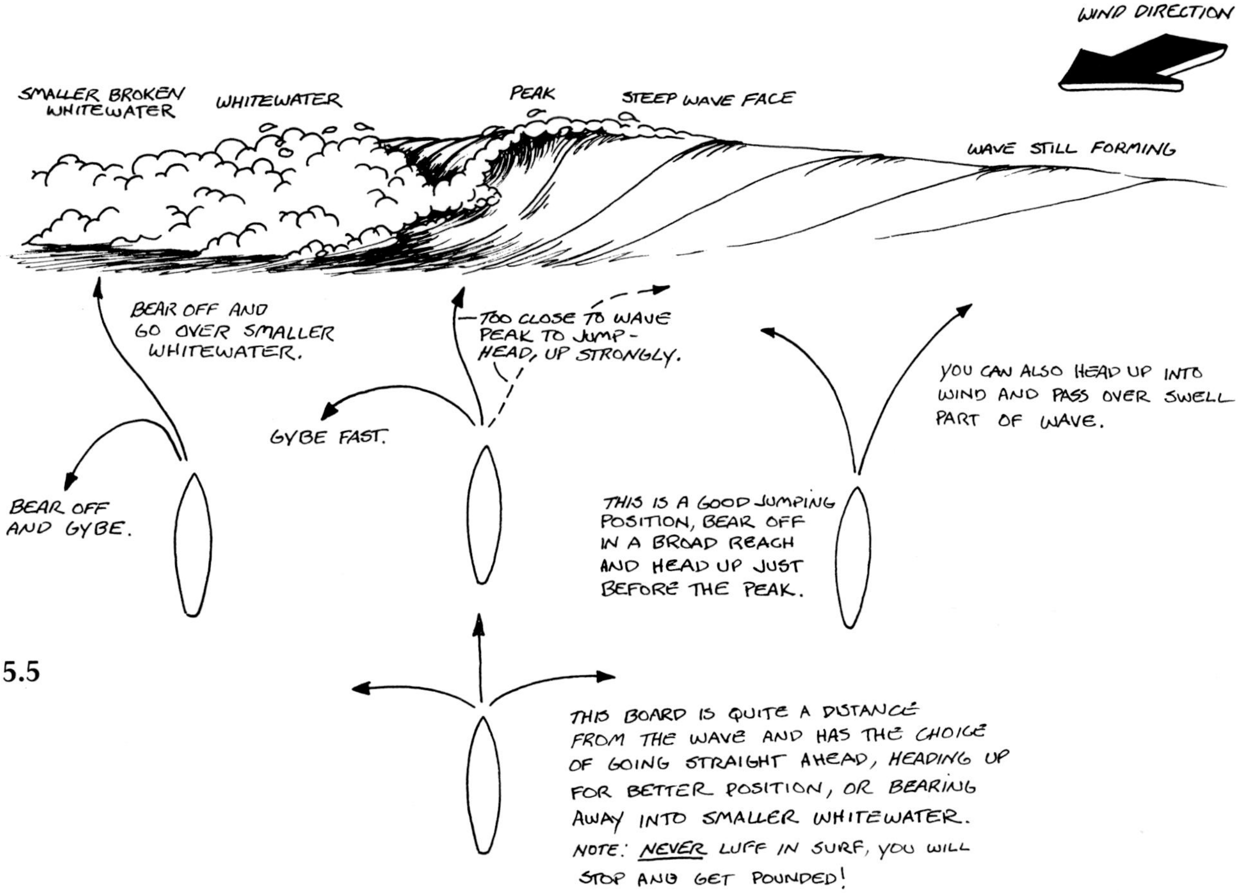

WIND DIRECTION

SMALLER BROKEN WHITEWATER   WHITEWATER   PEAK   STEEP WAVE FACE

WAVE STILL FORMING

BEAR OFF AND GO OVER SMALLER WHITEWATER.

— TOO CLOSE TO WAVE PEAK TO JUMP - HEAD, UP STRONGLY.

YOU CAN ALSO HEAD UP INTO WIND AND PASS OVER SWELL PART OF WAVE.

GYBE FAST.

BEAR OFF AND GYBE.

THIS IS A GOOD JUMPING POSITION, BEAR OFF IN A BROAD REACH AND HEAD UP JUST BEFORE THE PEAK.

5.5

THIS BOARD IS QUITE A DISTANCE FROM THE WAVE AND HAS THE CHOICE OF GOING STRAIGHT AHEAD, HEADING UP FOR BETTER POSITION, OR BEARING AWAY INTO SMALLER WHITEWATER.
NOTE: NEVER LUFF IN SURF, YOU WILL STOP AND GET POUNDED!

5.6

Wipeout

If you do wipe out in the surfline, the ideal position for your rig is to have the mast toward sea and the board toward shore. In this position, your sail acts as a drag, while the reverse position (i.e. the sail shoreward of the board) can easily result in a broken mast.

Over the years, I've broken dozens of masts, but stronger masts and sinking the mast tip under a breaking wave have saved a lot of potential mast casualties. I simply stand on the mast and grip it with both hands or grab the mast and stand on the sail toward the tip (Figure 5.7). Things happen fast at this point, and I usually grab whatever I can easily take hold of. The important thing is to sink the tip and sail, which allows water to flow over the sail and keep the board shoreward. Also, by hanging on to the sail tip, your body acts as an additional drag. Even if your rig is out of position, sinking the sail will cause it to rotate into the proper position as the wave passes.

I use this technique in big and small surf, deep and shallow water. However, in shallow water, I'm careful to stand on top of the sail so that my feet don't get ripped if the rig gets dragged across a reef.

One piece of equipment that helps when you're trying to sink a mast tip is the mast tip handle (Figure 5.8). Basically, it's a loop of nylon webbing hand-sewn to the tip of the mast sock. I use it mostly in larger surf and deeper water, where I can pull the mast under and not have to worry about hitting bottom. When a wave is about to break or when white water is approaching, I usually stand on my mast and then grab the handle.

In every case, what you're trying to avoid is the somersaulting effect that starts when a wave breaks under the mast and flips it shoreward, leaving the board to seaward. You can imagine the stresses that result when a mast gets jammed into the bottom and the

full force of the wave comes down on the board.

If the waves are breaking far apart when you wipe out, you should quickly and carefully attempt a water start or an uphaul start, depending on your equipment and the wind conditions. If this isn't possible, simply let the waves push you farther inside, where you can get it started again.

Now that we're done wiping out, let's go jump some waves.

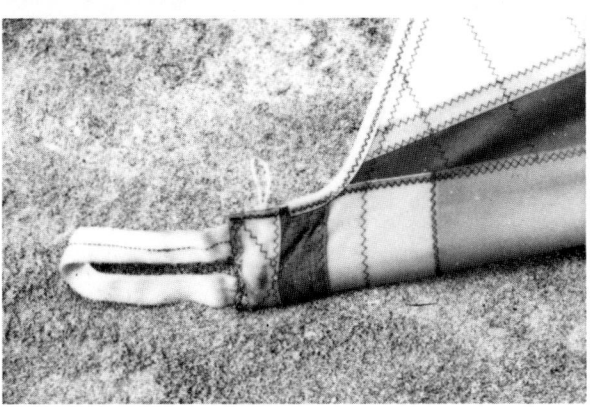

5.7

5.8

Jumping in Sideshore Winds

In sideshore conditions, you'll always be heading directly out through the surf on a beam reach. For this reason, jumping surf in these conditions is unlike chop jumping. With sideshore winds, it's no longer necessary to head up in order to gain maximum height on your jumps since you're already heading directly into the waves. This direct approach is exactly what you need in order to take full advantage of the steepness of the wave face. Imagine the thrill of hitting that face at top speed and getting launched skyward!

As always, the launch approach is critical. What you want to do is hit the lip so that the white water breaks just after your nose is over the top of the wave (Figure 5.9). Hitting the lip in this way lifts the board higher into the air much like the lip on a ski ramp (Figure 5.10). If your approach is too late, though, and the wave breaks under the back of the board as it's leaving the water, the resulting turbulence can push the tail up and send you into a nose dive. If you're later than this, the wave might even break on you, pushing your board over backward and leaving you to try again. Here, luck has a lot to do with whether or not you're successful. You can predict what the waves will do, but you can never tell what the wind will do. This is something you'll have to experiment with and something you should never expect to have completely wired. This is okay, though. After all, pitting your skills against the unpredictable challenges that the wind and water have to offer is what this sport is all about and what gives it so much of its excitement.

The only problem with arriving too early is that you won't catch the wave in its most vertical phase. This means that you won't jump as high as if you'd hit it just right. However, arriving early is just fine if you're going for a longer, faster flying jump. In fact, if you're in waves breaking close together, you'll want to make such jumps in order to maintain forward speed so that you can make it over a larger wave approaching from farther outside.

5.10

5.9

To make a long jump, simply aim for the shoulder of the wave where it's less steep. Then, follow the same steps for performing a long jump in chop (Figure 5.11). Save high jumps for those bigger outside waves.

5.11

5.12

5.13

Upside Down Jumps

When going for a high jump, it's important that you keep the rig pulled over on top of you in order to allow the sail to act as a parachute. If you level off too soon, you'll drop down nose first and wipe out as soon as you hit the water—and hit it you will. This is why you'll see performance sailors who are doing high jumps sailing through the air completely upside down, although it's not essential that you go totally upside down as Matt Schweitzer does in Figure 5.12. Besides having a great time, their aim with this type of maneuver is to keep from landing nose first in the water. The higher you go, the more upside down you'll want to get in order to avoid leveling off too soon (Figure 5.13). Remember, never land flat. Often you'll end up landing nose first after a high jump, as Robby Nash demonstrates in Figures 5.14–14E.

5.14B

5.14A

5.14

5.14C

5.14D

5.14E

When you first begin jumping, you may not want to jump very high. If this is the case, or if you sense that you don't have full control at takeoff, simply luff the sail as you climb the wave for the jump. This will slow you down and limit your jumping momentum.

As your wave-jumping skills improve and you learn to enjoy the pleasures of weightlessness, you'll probably want to try putting your board into some radical positions, like a mule kick or an incredibly high, upside down jump.

Once you've gotten trimming in the air wired, you can do a mule kick simply by kicking your feet and leg to windward while concentrating with your upper body to maintain proper sail trim (Figure 5.15). At this point, your board is free to do whatever you tell it to—as long as you stay sailing (Figure 5.16). The big thing here is to keep your board in a consistent sailing position by trimming the sail and knowing when to bring your board and feet under your body in time for a decent landing. Nobody said learning how to mule kick wasn't going to take some practice.

5.15

5.16

5.17

Most of these air acrobatics are just free-form acts of self-expression. Instead of riding the board level, the object is to see how radical you can get by throwing the board around while you're sailing in a weightless state. Remember, however, if you haven't leveled things out enough to make a controlled landing by the time the board is ready to hit the water, you'd better be prepared to bail (Figure 5.17)!

Jumping in Sideoffshore Winds

It's still possible to jump in sideoffshore winds, but you can no longer hit the wave head on at full speed. This is because trying to meet a wave head on in these conditions puts you on a broad reach, and this point of sail won't generate the power you'll need to make it up the vertical wave face, hit the lip, and really take off. Also, it's very difficult to control a board in midair when you're as far off the wind as a head-on approach in sideoffshore winds will put you. So what you've got to do is hit the wave at an angle in order to ensure that you'll be jumping on a beam reach. This will give you more power, although it's going to cramp your style in terms of getting high off the water with your jumps. The reason for this is that an angled, or "indirect," approach won't give you as vertical a takeoff from the wave face as a head-on approach.

Another difficulty with sideoffshore winds is that when you're coming down from a jump you'll experience wind turbulence, since the breaking wave will be between your sail and the wind. This causes funny things to happen to the rig when you're jumping, and it requires a constant readiness on your part to sheet way in or out in order to adjust to major wind shifts and keep the board riding level.

Gusts are another common problem with sideoffshore winds. If a wind shift hits you in the form of a lift (i.e. blows at you from the shore), you'll be oversheeted instantly and heading on a broader reach than the beam reach you were on. To counter this, you'll have to sheet out immediately with your aft hand and then head up to the correct heading in order to regain proper trim. Sometimes a wind shift will be so drastic that you'll have to let go completely with your aft hand and luff for an instant in order to avoid being launched over the board's bow. If a wind shift hits you in the form of a header (i.e. blows at you from an onshore direction), you'll have to sheet in instantly with your aft hand and lean the mast way forward in order to bear away so that you can avoid getting caught pointing too high into the wind. In a strong onshore gust, it will take a lot of muscle to avoid being thrown into the water.

When jumping, try to avoid bearing off in midair. The danger in doing so is that you'll land on a very broad reach and then immediately sink. So don't tip the board to leeward very much or do anything else that might make you bear off in the air. Whenever possible jump on a beam reach and hit the wave at a forty-five-degree angle to the sideoffshore wind. However, if the wave is big or steep or has broken into thick, white water, it's essential that you hit it head on at a ninety-degree angle at the last possible moment in order to make it over the top. Remember, never hit a large breaking wave broadside. The trick here is to pop a wheelie on a broad reach so that the nose hits the wave head on and still lifts you up and over the foam. Then, immediately head up again to a beam reach to be properly trimmed in the air.

Jumping in Sideonshore Winds

In sideonshore winds, you must sail out through the surf at an angle again in order to stay on a beam reach. To make it over waves, you should head up at the last possible second and hit the wave head on. Once you're airborne, you've got to get the board to bear off as you do in onshore winds, only not as far. You'll be able to do this by tilting the board way over to leeward, leaning the mast forward, and pushing downwind with your forward foot while pulling with your aft—just as you would in onshore conditions or when jumping chop.

5.18

5.18A

115

5.19

Lollipop

On occasion, it's possible to be heading in the same direction as the waves and chop and still pull off a small jump, called a lollipop (Figures 5.18–18A). The secret to making a good lollipop is to be tearing along on a beam reach and to find a piece of chop or a ripple on the face of a wave that's moving more against you than with you. When you see a piece of chop or a ripple like this, head up to hit it, lift off, and then bear off in the air to a beam reach (Figure 5.19). Basically, this is chop jumping in reverse and just another high-speed trick to try.

6. Surfing

Once you've gotten the hang of riding your board in strong winds, you may want to take it out into the surf. But before you do, learning the "rules of the surf" is an absolute must.

Rules of the Surf

As much fun as surfing is, it can also be dangerous. The biggest danger really isn't the waves themselves (unless they're huge!) but others like yourself who are playing in the surfline, (swimmers, divers, board surfers, body surfers, and other sailors). In order to avoid collisions, wave riders have created a set of "rules of the surf" as a courtesy to one another and to anyone else enjoying the waves. These rules are as follows:

1. Have respect for anyone you encounter in the water.

2. Because all other wave riders playing in the surf are less maneuverable than a sailboard, the sailboarder must always yield the right of way.

3. No sailboard should drop into a wave that has boardsurfers or swimmers trying to ride it and should yield right of way at all times.

4. The first sailor on a wave or swell has the rights to that wave or swell over any other sailor, but not over surfers or others in the surfline.

5. If two sailors catch the same wave at the same time, the upwind sailor has the right of way and the downwind sailor should get off the wave or stay well clear. Remember how fast a performance board can travel (twenty to thirty miles per hour with a quick gust), so it's important to give other sailors a very wide berth.

6. If you feel that you have the right of way on a wave, hail any other sailors so they know your intentions.

7. The sailor on starboard tack has right of way as long as he holds his course. Remember, we are "sail" boards, and in

the event of a serious collision we'll be judged in court by the rules of sailing.

8. The sailor riding in should avoid trying any radical maneuvers near or in front of another rider trying to get out. If you want to take a risk, do it at your own expense, not someone else's.

9. Always look over your downwind shoulder before jibing in order to avoid turning into someone behind you and to leeward. This is always a blind spot when jibing.

10. A board in the process of turning or jibing has no rights.

Once you've memorized these rules, the next step is to choose a spot where you can begin wave riding. Obviously, picking a spot that's well suited to your abilities as a beginner will make learning a much more pleasurable experience.

Caution: Choosing a spot that's too challenging for you can make learning not only difficult but frightening and dangerous.

Choosing a Surf Spot

As we saw in the last chapter, all waves aren't the same. Some are mushy and slow, while others are hollow and fast. As a beginner, the best waves to practice on are those of the "mushier" variety. For the beginner, things happen too fast on a hollow wave. The type of beach a wave breaks on is also important. There are four basic types: reefs, rock bottoms, sandbars, and points.

Reefs are found mostly in tropical locales and are not the greatest places to learn, although they offer the nicest and easiest waves to ride once you've gained some experience. Coming into contact with reefs should be avoided, since they're sharp enough to cut you and your sails. This means that you've got to be especially cautious when launching or maneuvering in order to avoid wiping out and hitting bottom. Also, reef breaks usually produce hollower, more powerful waves. This isn't always the case, however, and deep-water reefs do provide the beginner with two major pluses: they normally have deep-water channels where waves won't be breaking, and they usually have a "deep spot" on the inside where you can turn around in flat water without waves breaking on the beach. This makes getting in and out through the surf and jibing inside considerably easier if the waves are big or breaking close together.

Like reefs, rock bottoms also produce fast-breaking waves. And while there's less danger of getting cut should you come in contact with this type of bottom, it's still not advisable to go bouncing off one after a wipeout! Also, you've got to be careful to avoid stepping on sea urchins and sharp rocks when launching. Other than this, rock bottoms are fine for beginners, as long as the waves aren't too big or too hollow or breaking too close to shore (waves that "close out" close to shore are terrible for surfing, since it's almost impossible to jibe around quickly enough once your ride is over).

Sandbars are the ideal surfing spots for beginners, provided they're well formed so that the waves are peaking instead of closing out. Sandbars normally (although not always) provide for slower waves, so there's far less danger of getting hurt should you hit bottom.

Point breaks are rare but often provide the longest and best rides. Points can have any of the bottom types I've just described and can therefore produce waves of any speed. The biggest problem with point breaks is that they seldom provide the wind conditions you need. For example, if the wind blows sideshore off a point, it's generally too light (because it's being blocked by the point) to give you the speed you'll need unless the point is very low,

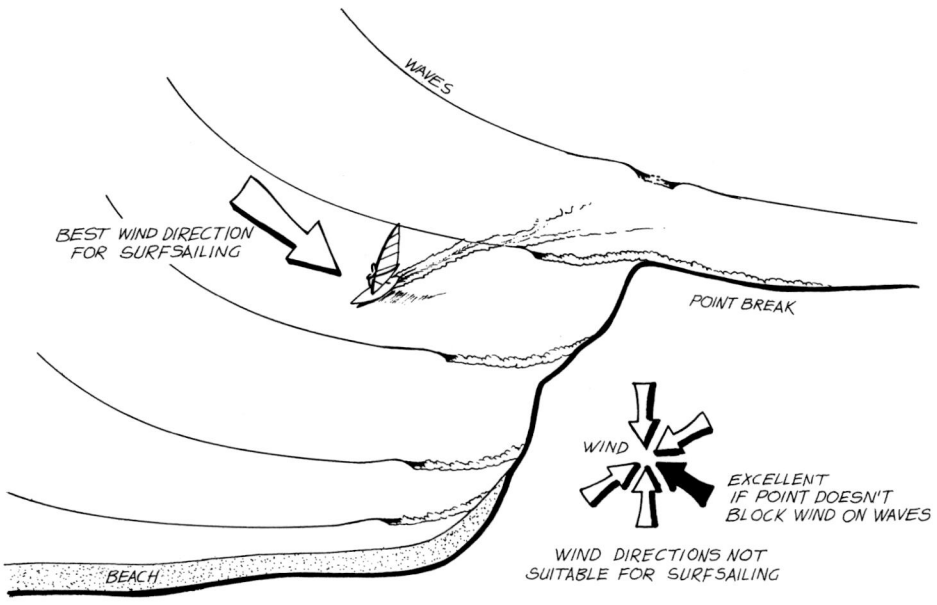

POINT DIAGRAM

allowing wind to come across it. And since you can't surf in a direct onshore or offshore wind, the only winds that'll work are those blowing from the ocean toward the point— i.e., forty-five degrees onshore to the waves. If you can find these winds and the right point, though, you're in for a good time (Figure 6.1).

Points provide for exceptionally long rides, since a wave's shoulder will peel off evenly as it follows the wave around the point.

Once you've found the surf spot that's best suited to your abilities, the next step is to start studying the conditions.

Studying the Conditions

If you're a newcomer to the ocean, it's a good idea to learn a few things about its behavior and then study the conditions before you go out. Remember the following:

1. Waves are generated by storms at sea. Learn how to follow storms on the weather map and how to watch them form. This can help you figure out how strong the current is and in what direction it will run in the surfline. Following storms can also help you tell when it's time to throw your board on top of the car and head for the beach.

2. Tidal changes can have a great effect on how and where a wave will break. Normally, lower tides mean faster-breaking waves, and higher tides mean mushier ones. So it's always a good idea to know when the tide is coming in or going out. If you're a beginner, it may be wise to avoid lower tides until your reactions improve. In some areas of the world, though, tides differ very little, if at all. At those places, you take what's available. In other places, a reef or sandbar that's under water at high tide will be dry at low tide.

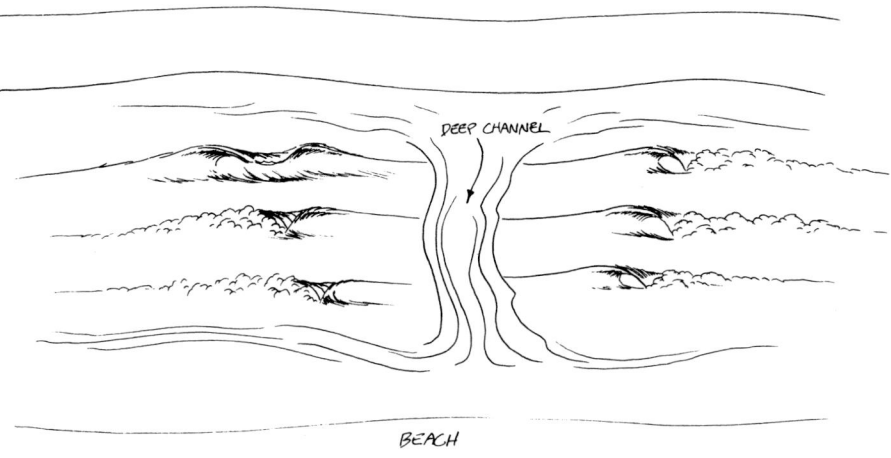

6.2

DEEP CHANNEL

BEACH

3. One good way to check tidal changes is to keep an eye on whether the water level is rising or falling in relationship to exposed rocks or parts of a reef. At some spots, a high tide can be readily detected by the fact that no rocks or parts of a reef are exposed. Low tides, on the other hand, can often be determined by the fact that rocks or large parts of a reef have been left exposed by the receding water.

4. Know the area where the waves are breaking and keep aware of your position relative to it.

5. Locate the channel if there is one. If the waves are big, sailing out through the channel is better than chancing it through the surf (Figure 6.2).

6. Water that flows into the surfline has to get back out. It does so through any channel available. This movement of water back out to sea is what's commonly known as a "rip tide." If you should get caught in a rip, don't attempt to swim directly back in. Instead, swim sideways to the beach and with the prevailing current until you're out of it. Then swim in. Never try to fight straight against current; you'll only tire yourself out and get nowhere.

6.3

WIND

SIDESHORE GOING RIGHT
BOTTOM TURN
SPEED TRIM
ROLLER COASTER
SLASHBACK
OFF THE LIP
CUTBACK

6.3A

WIND

SIDESHORE GOING LEFT
BOTTOM TURN
SPEED TRIM
CUTBACK
LIMITED OFF THE LIP
LIMITED SLASHBACK
LIMITED ROLLER COASTER

Wind Conditions

Of all the conditions that will affect you on the water, the first and most important things to consider are wind direction and wind speed. These will determine whether you should or shouldn't go out, whether you can ride both right and left or in only one direction. They'll also determine what types of maneuvers you'll be able to perform.

Sideshore

As we saw in the last chapter, sideshore winds are the best winds for jumping and surfing. When going right in sideshore winds, where the winds are blowing from right to left, you can perform all of the maneuvers listed in Figure 6.3. Going left in the same conditions is also possible, although a little more limiting, since you must head fairly high into the wind. For this reason, when going left in sideshore winds that are blowing from right to left, you can only perform the maneuvers listed in Figure 6.3A.

If winds are blowing from left to right in a sideshore condition, then the situation is reversed. Going left becomes preferred, while going right becomes more difficult.

Sideonshore

If winds are blowing from right to left in sideonshore conditions, the preferred direction for riding a wave is left. (Remember that "right" and "left" are as viewed from offshore when determining wind conditions, whereas "right"and "left" in wave riding is determined by the rider facing shore. When a surfer is going left on a wave, he looks to be going right to someone on shore.) Here, you'll be headed mainly on a beam reach, whereas if you go right, you'll be headed nearly or past downwind and won't have any speed or control. In this sort of situation, you'd be relying solely on the wave for your speed, since it would be able to push you along faster than the wind. So when going right, you can fully perform all the possible surfing maneuvers frontside (Figure 6.4), whereas if you go left, you'll only be able to perform the maneuvers listed in Figure 6.4A, like a backside off the lip (Figures 6.5–5B).

6.4

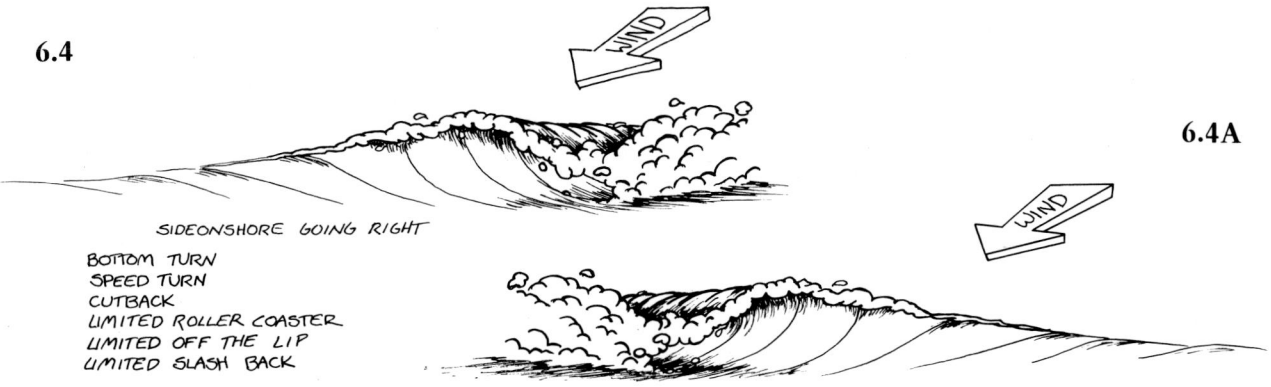

SIDEONSHORE GOING RIGHT

BOTTOM TURN
SPEED TURN
CUTBACK
LIMITED ROLLER COASTER
LIMITED OFF THE LIP
LIMITED SLASH BACK

6.4A

SIDEONSHORE GOING LEFT

BOTTOM TURN
SPEED TURN
CUT BACK
SLASHBACK
ROLLER COASTER
OFF THE LIP

It's also important to keep in mind that the more onshore the wind is blowing, the more difficult it becomes to perform offwind maneuvers and the easier it becomes to perform close-hauled maneuvers. The reverse is also true: the more offshore the wind is blowing, the easier it becomes to perform offwind maneuvers and the harder it becomes to perform close-hauled ones.

If winds are blowing from left to right in sideonshore conditions, the situation is reversed. Going right becomes preferred, because you're closer to the wind, and going left gets more difficult, because you're too far off the wind.

6.5

6.5B

6.5A

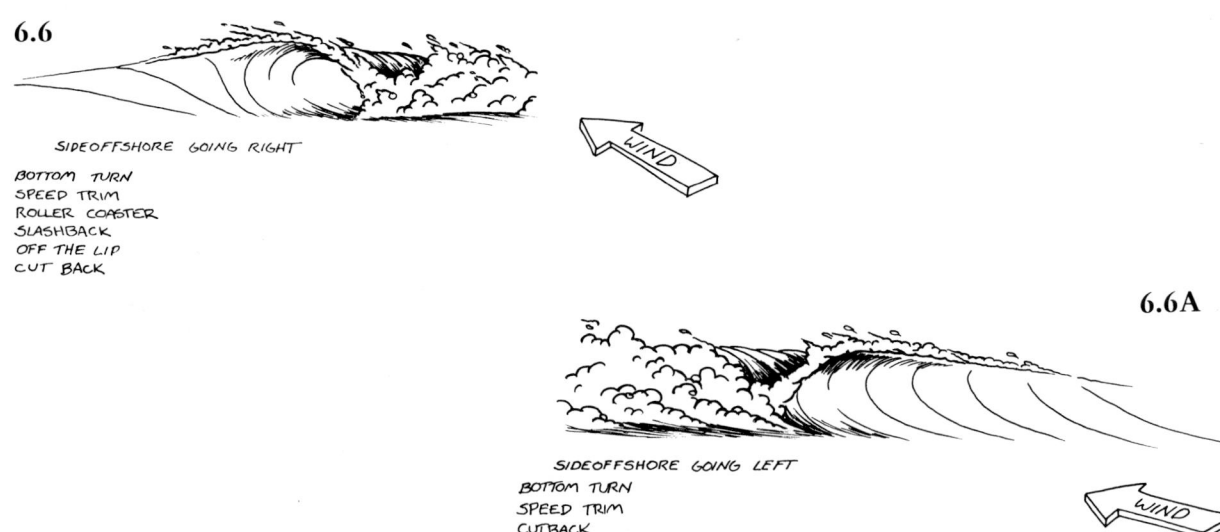

6.6

SIDEOFFSHORE GOING RIGHT

BOTTOM TURN
SPEED TRIM
ROLLER COASTER
SLASHBACK
OFF THE LIP
CUT BACK

6.6A

SIDEOFFSHORE GOING LEFT
BOTTOM TURN
SPEED TRIM
CUTBACK
LIMITED ROLLER COASTER
LIMITED SLASHBACK
LIMITED OFF THE LIP

Sideoffshore

If winds are blowing from right to left in sideoffshore conditions, the preferred direction for riding a wave is right. Going right, you're mainly headed on a beam reach, whereas going left you'll be headed nearly dead into the wind, making it impossible to turn up the face. When going right, you can safely perform all the possible surfing maneuvers (Figure 6.6), whereas if you go left, you'll only be able to perform the maneuvers listed in Figure 6.6A. And remember, if it gets too far offshore, you'll have difficulty surfing at all.

If the winds are blowing from left to right in a sideoffshore condition, the reverse is true.

Once you've sized up the wind and determined which way you want to ride the waves and which maneuvers you'll readily be able to do, you're ready to head out, turn around, and ride a wave back in. As they say, now's the time to go for it!

P.S. Don't let this section confuse you. The best way to understand wind conditions is to get out on the water and feel them!

Turning Around

After you've powered out through the foam and waves (Chapter 5), the safest place to jibe is way out past the surfline, where you can jibe in any manner you wish. If you want to turn around very close to the surfline, however, you'll want to perform what's known as a "jibe takeoff." This type of maneuver is done almost exactly like a high-wind power jibe. The only difference is that you try to time your turn across the face of an oncoming swell or wave in such a way that you actually get pushed out of the turn (Figure 6.7). This sort of turn is similar to a banked turn in car racing—turning your board at such a sharp angle causes it to get rocketed out of the turn at tremendous speed. Because it does, though, you've got to be prepared to release the sail sooner for your jibe, whether you plan on doing a regular jibe or a duck jibe.

Riding Back In

In the beginning, the object of wave riding is to follow a wave for as long as you can and avoid wiping out. As you improve, though, your objectives will change. Basically, you should have three goals:

1. Stay on the wave as long as possible.

2. Stay as close to the curl or lip as possible.

3. Do as many radical maneuvers in tight sections as possible and do so with grace and style.

The last of these objectives is what performance windsurfing is all about—developing a style that's both radical and smooth. Performing outrageous tricks that look effortless and easy is the challenge. In this sense, the goal in surfing is the same as that in freestyling. Wave riding provides endless variety—and so also endless discovery and challenge.

6.7

Dropping In

Dropping into a wave is a total rush. As it builds behind you, your tail will slowly lift, your bow will drop, and you'll begin to accelerate. Keeping in mind that you want to stay as close to the curl as possible and need to have your daggerboard totally retracted if you have one, there are a number of ways to drop in.

Ideally, you'll time your descent so that, as the curl begins to break, it's right behind you. If it breaks way behind you, you'll either have to luff up a lot to let the wave catch you or you'll have to fade toward its peak. If it breaks at nearly the same time that you're dropping in, you'll have to negotiate a steep drop and try to avoid pearling at the bottom.

The late drop is by far the most dangerous one but fortunately not necessary on performance boards, since they can catch a wave way outside before it breaks. Nevertheless, late drops do occasionally occur, and you should know what to do. The big danger, of course, is sticking the nose straight into the bottom of a wave, known as a pearl (Figure 6.8).

To avoid a pearl, don't sheet in—remember that in jumping you sheet in to bring the nose down. This is exactly what you don't want to happen. If you really come in late, say, charging over the breaking lip, backwind. This is done by pushing the boom way out so that it catches the wind on its leeward side, causing the board to slow and its nose to stick up in the air. Backwinding like this can also help you avoid dropping into a wave you don't want—either because someone else already has it or because it has poor shape and you aren't sure you can make it.

Whichever way you drop in, you'll experience a dramatic increase in power and a slight change in wind direction. Apparent wind accounts for this. To deal with it, you may either have to push the mast forward and sheet in or sheet out in order to reduce excess pressure. Which of these you do will depend on the situation and how much wind you can handle. One thing to keep in mind here is the role that sail area plays in maintaining control. For example, if you've got things just under control on the way out but can't handle the increases in apparent wind when riding in, you probably need to flatten your sail or switch to a smaller one.

6.8

6.9

6.9A

6.9B

6.9C

Bottom Turn

Once you hit the bottom of the wave, you'll want to make a bottom turn to climb back up its face (Figures 6.9–9D). A bottom turn is done in pretty much the same way as a jibe, except that you've really got to carve the rail in deep to keep from "spinning out" at high speed. How much you sheet in or sheet out once you hit the bottom depends mainly on how fast you're moving and how much speed your board can handle before it begins to spin out. If you hit the bottom going full speed in high winds, chances are you'll need to over-trim (Figure 6.10) in order to reduce the danger of wiping out. But if you drop in on a mushy wave in a lighter, sideonshore wind, you may need to trim out for speed throughout the entire turn (Figure 6.11).

Another thing you'll need to consider when doing a bottom turn is how tight or "drawn out" you want to make it. If the wave is very peaky and the shoulder isn't breaking very fast, you'll want to make a very tight bottom turn so that you don't outrun the wave (Figure 6.12). If the wave is breaking fast, though, and you can see a section forming ahead (an area where the shoulder is higher than in an another part of the wave, and consequently going to break sooner), you may want to draw your turn out, projecting your board way down the line.

In the former instance, where the wave is peaking, you can come up to the top and do either a slashback, a cutback, or an off the lip. But if you have oversheeted for a fast bottom turn, keep in mind that you must open the sail back up to a broad reach or more to pull off one of these turns at the top (Figures 6.9–9D).

6.9D

6.10

6.11

6.12

Slashback

A slashback is a sharp, pivoting turn off the top executed just down the shoulder from the breaking lip where the board is turned back around toward the wave (Figure 6.13). To make one, you shift the pressure you're exerting with your feet to the opposite rail, really pushing on the inside rail with your aft foot in order to turn the board back down the wave. The further aft you place your foot, the more radical your turn will be. As you are turning, you'll also have to sheet the sail way out, especially if the winds are sideonshore or sideoffshore. Once the slashback is completed, you should drop down again and prepare for another bottom turn.

6.13

Cutback

6.14

A cutback is a drawn out turn done off the top, fairly far down from the breaking lip (Figure 6.14). It's a turn that's meant to take you back toward the more powerful, breaking parts of the wave. How sharply you'll want to cut back will depend on how far out on the shoulder you went and how steep the wave is. The steeper the wave, the more sharply you can turn on its face without stalling out.

Perhaps the most difficult part of pulling off these maneuvers is keeping in mind that you have two power sources to draw upon—the wind and the wave. When winds are light and unfavorable, you'll need to rely more upon the wave in order to perform well. When winds are heavy and favorable, though, and the waves are breaking either slowly or imperfectly, you'll need to rely more upon the wind.

When the wind is your main source of power, trimming your sail correctly at all times is essential. So when you're turning always keep in mind where the wind is coming from in relation to your heading.

If you were going right in sideshore winds at Hookipa, for example, you'd drop in on a beam reach, bottom turn onto a broad reach, and then cut back onto a close reach (Figure 6.15). So if you're ever in need of more power, make certain that you sheet your sail to follow each of these course changes as you perform your turns on the wave face. If you don't need power, simply over- or undersheet as necessary in order to maintain control.

Another type of cutback is called a "round house cutback." Here, you cut back off the curl heading away from it instead of off the shoulder and into the curl (Figure 6.16).

6.15

6.16

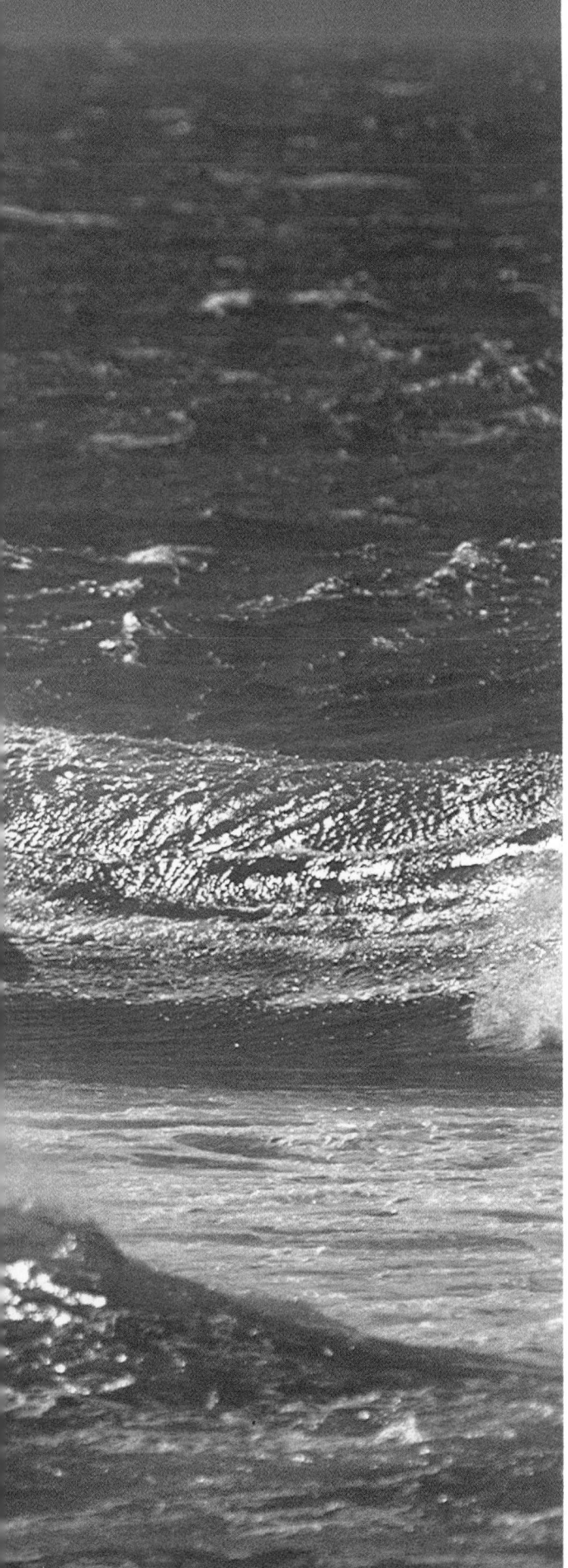

Off the Lip

One of the most advanced maneuvers you can do is an "off the lip" (Figure 6.17). An off the lip is done by making a bottom turn that brings you back up to the top of the wave at just the right moment so that the nose of your board smacks the lip as it's breaking and then gets thrown back down the wave face (Figures 6.5–5B). How successfull your off the lip is depends on how well you time your bottom turn. You put pressure on the inside rail with your aft foot to pull off the bottom turn and then level things out until the board hits the lip. Then you put lots of pressure on your aft foot to pivot back down the wave and keep the nose from pearling as you drop back down. Sometimes they even get airborne off the lip and have to make a landing from midair (Figures 6.18–18C).

6.17

6.18

6.18A

6.18C

6.18B

Trimming

In either unfavorable winds or very fast waves with long shoulders, it's also important to know how to trim for speed. In a speed trim, you pick a line down the wave and go straight rather than climb up and down the face in a series of roller coasters (Figure 6.19). At the Pipeline in Hawaii, which has very fast waves, boardsurfers like Jerry Lopez trim for most of the ride so they can surf inside the tube. Instead of dropping in and doing a sharp bottom turn off the lip, he drops in and turns his board toward the wave face, letting it push him along sideways.

When the winds are unfavorable (for example, when you're going left on a sideshore wind blowing from right to left), you'll have to do a lot of trimming to keep up with a fast-moving shoulder. So instead of dropping and climbing a lot, you'd trim most of the wave. Even when winds are favorable, though, you may need to trim. A good trim will help you reach a breaking section and then enable you to drop down and do a bottom turn around it.

Whenever you're trimming, the important thing to remember is that you'll lose the trim if you drop below the top two-thirds of the wave. The point of trimming is to keep heading down at a slight angle, allowing the forward motion of the wave to lift you up and push you forward at the same time. If you go too high, the wave will throw you over, and if you go too low, you'll lose its power and have to turn back up toward its "juice center."

Wave riding is a dance. At first, your moves will be limited and your style necessarily cautious and unaggressive. As you go along, though, observing the styles and techniques of the masters, you'll start to develop your own unique way of expressing yourself. With wave riding, there's nothing better than time spent on the water or time spent watching others on the water.

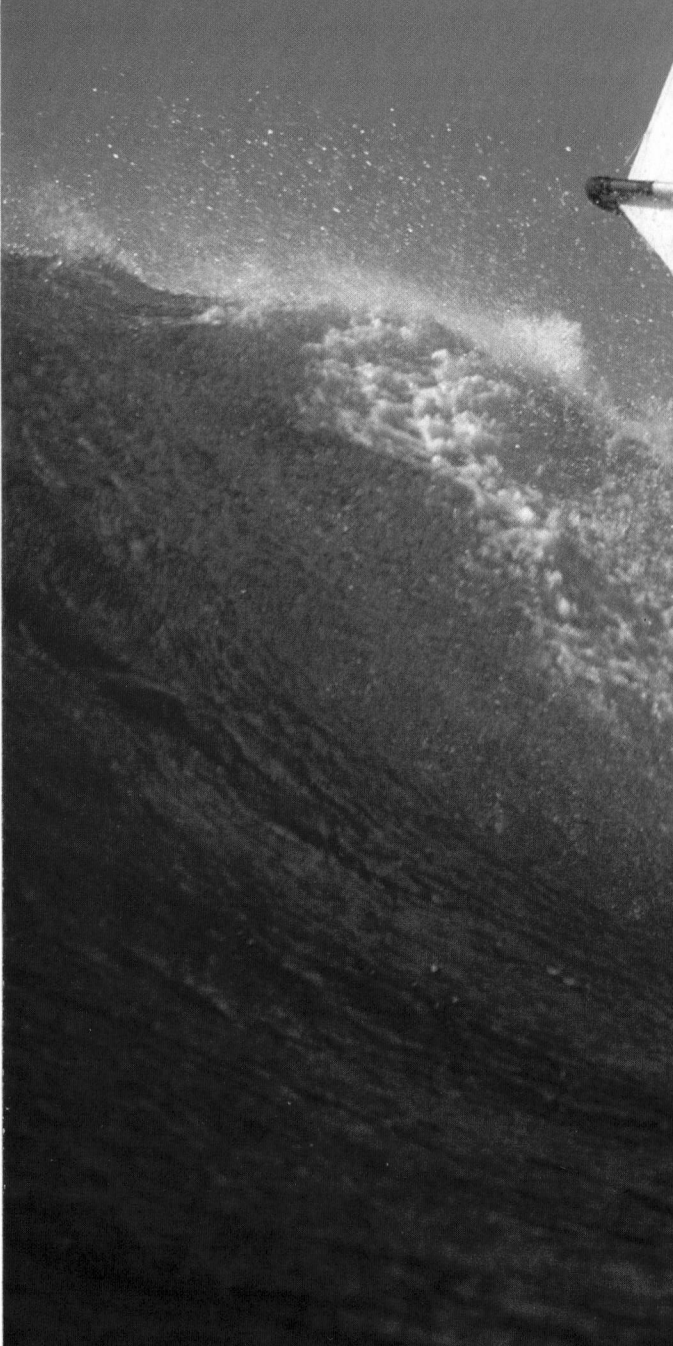

6.19

Tips

Once you've finished riding a wave, you'll want to sail in to where things are calm enough that you can turn around and head out for another ride. When you do, it's important to consider positioning. After you've turned around, you'll want to be headed out

either toward the channel or directly toward the peaks, depending upon whether you want to jump or not. This may mean heading way up at the end of a ride, so that when you jibe you're going out through the middle of the surfline, or it may mean falling way off so you can avoid it. All of this depends, of course, on where you're surfing. In any event, avoid jibing in shallow water because you run the risk

of tearing your fin off. It's also a good idea to try to stay upwind as much as possible, since this makes heading back out easier. So when heading in, take advantage of the wave's or the foam's ability to help you generate speed with apparent wind. With this extra boost, you can often work pretty far upwind and then jibe around and be headed directly back out on a perfect beam reach.

7. Choosing a Board and Fins

If I could honestly tell you that choosing a performance board is easy, I would. But it isn't. A number of factors need to be looked at carefully, and no one factor can be considered separately without taking into account the rest. It's simply not possible to decide on a board length without considering its width; to decide on rail shapes without considering board thickness; to decide on a tail shape without considering tail width, and on and on. You'll need to understand the effects of factors that alter board performance, combined with an ability to juggle them properly so that you end up with a board that suits your needs best.

In the following pages I will try to point out the pros and cons of many aspects of board and fin design. When reading this material, try to bear in mind that choosing a board is a matter of compromises. Whenever you get something you usually give something away. There is no such thing as a perfect board—only a perfect relationship between the board, its rider, and the elements.

Much of the technical information and theory presented in this chapter may be confusing, so don't get hung up trying to understand everything here at once. Some things just won't become clear to you until you've spent some time on the water and experienced the problems I'll be talking about. Also, don't expect to read this chapter and then go design your own board. The people who build and sell them can usually steer you in the right direction if they treasure your business. The following information is provided simply to give you some background on what's what in hull and fin design theory.

Plastic Hulls

Performance boards are constructed in a number of different ways, and certain types of construction are better suited to the needs of particular individuals than others.

The most popular type of plastic hull construction is polyethylene (Figure 7.1), a method perfected by the man who started it all, Hoyle Schweitzer of Windsurfer International. These

7.1

7.2.

hulls are rotation-molded in a closed mold, which is heated until polyethylene chips melt and cover the inside of the mold to form a hollow hull shell. These hollow hull shells are then placed in a retainer mold and filled with foam. Hulls constructed in this manner can withstand more impact and abuse than any other type of hull. When a polyethylene hull actually gets a ding, though, it requires a time-consuming repair. As far as nonskid surface is concerned, polyethylene hulls are great—they provide plenty of traction for your feet.

Another popular type of plastic hull construction is ABS (Figure 7.2). ABS boards are vacuum-formed and then bonded together, with the foam and the sealed edges acting as the bonding agent. ABS boards can't withstand abuse as well as polyethylene boards, but when they actually do need repair they are a lot easier to fix. ABS boards don't provide the optimum nonskid but usually have a very nice finish to them.

All in all, plastic boards (whatever plastic they're made with) have the following advantages:

1. Durability. They are carefree to use and long-lasting and have good resale value, especially if you buy a known and respected brand.

2. Price. A plastic board is generally less expensive than a professionally hand-crafted custom fiberglass board.

3. Shape. Most plastic boards are well shaped. The manufacturer has undertaken extensive research and design to be certain the board was a good performer for the conditions it was designed and worthy of a costly mold. Fiberglass boards, on the other hand, vary from the great to the disastrous.

4. Test sail. If you can test sail a plastic board and like it, you can purchase an identical model and be confident it will perform to your satisfaction.

5. Many plastic board manufacturers have a wide range of boards that suit a number of different needs. Also, many of them make nice compromise shapes that will perform well in a wide variety of conditions.

6. Plastic boards are getting lighter and stiffer each year, making them more and more desirable for the sailor who doesn't need a custom hull shape.

Despite the above advantages, plastic boards have two disadvantages: they are heavier than fiberglass boards (although they get lighter each year with new materials and new methods of construction), and their shapes are not as finely tuned (which will always be the case). Increases in weight naturally decrease performance—acceleration, jumping, and overall speed.

All in all, a plastic hull, though not the ultimate in performance, is very suitable to get you started in short board sailing. It will be some time before you'll need or want a custom fiberglass board.

Fiberglass Hulls

Presently, fiberglass is the material demanding windsurfers most prefer for board construction. A foam blank can be shaped to meet your exact needs and then covered with any number of glass layers to produce as light or strong a hull as you desire; you can also decorate it in any way you like. A fiberglass hull can be light, stiff, colorful, and finely tuned—leading to the highest possible performance and personal aesthetic pleasure. In Figure 7.3, Matt Schweitzer is pictured with his "quiver" of fiberglass performance boards.

The main disadvantage of fiberglass hulls is that they are easy to scratch or ding and need to be handled with greater care than polyethylene hulls. Fiberglass hulls are also more expensive than polyethylene hulls, and it's easy to purchase a bad one if you aren't fairly knowledgeable about hull shapes (see below) and what a top-quality glass job should look like. Such is usually not the case with reputable polyethylene hulls, which are designed by experts and thoroughly tested before being put into production.

Perhaps the best insurance against getting a poor fiberglass hull is to ask around and to read the windsurfing magazines carefully in order to learn who the best designers and manufacturers are. In particular, make certain that your shaper is more of a sailboard shaper than a surfboard shaper. Surfboards travel much more slowly than sailboards and by a different power source; consequently, surfboard shapers are not always familiar enough with the hydrodynamic theory which governs the performance of sailboard hull shapes.

7.3

When actually inspecting the construction, be certain to ask which type of foam blank was used in shaping the board. This is critical, since foam blank quality varies considerably. Presently, the best foam blanks are manufactured by Clark Foam. If the board you're considering isn't made from a Clark blank, ask around until you're certain that the blank it's made from is of comparable quality.

The best glass jobs are done with either "S" or "K" glass. These glasses cost a bit more but are well worth it since more time is spent actually weaving the cloth. In terms of strength-to-weight ratio, "S" or "K" glass is superior to the standard "E" glass used in constructing surfboards. Because S glass is lighter and has much more tensile strength than E glass the E glass board is less likely to

break in half. But in terms of impact strength, i.e., dings and shatters, there is no difference at all between S and E glass. K glass has less tensile strength but much higher impact strength than either E or S glass.

Another thing to consider is how well the board has been reinforced at stress points. So make certain that the tail, deck, straps, fin boxes, and skegs are thoroughly reinforced with extra layers of glass.

One thing you'll notice when shopping for a board, whether plastic or glass, is that cost varies considerably. If you are inclined to buy a cheaper product, a word of warning: generally, you get what you pay for. If you want quality, which always means more enjoyable sailing and a more dependable product with higher resale value, you are probably going to have to pay for it.

Length

Greater length means greater stability and less maneuverability at any speed. I can't generalize beyond this because the width of a board also plays a considerable role in determining how much planing surface it has and consequently how well it will perform a turn under various conditions.

I can say with confidence, however, that a board nine to ten feet long (normally called a floater) is appropriate for beginning performance sailors of average size (between 150 and 170 pounds). Such a board (if shaped properly for your weight) should be floaty enough to enable you to uphaul the sail and get under way in light airs and yet still allow you to carve fast rail turns, jump chop, and ride small waves. Of course, if you are more experienced and plan on spending a lot of time in the surf, you'll probably want a board between eight and nine feet in length (normally called a semisinker). Such a board will give you plenty of maneuverability in the surf and all the thrill you'll need or want when reaching in a solid wind. A board which you can't uphaul at all is called a sinker, strictly for high winds and large waves.

To determine the proper length for your board, you have to consider carefully the three W's: your sailing weight, the wind velocity, and the water surface conditions. For example, if the area you sail in seldom blows over eighteen knots and there's seldom any surf to ride, buying a sinker would be foolish, unless of course you "need" it for the roof of your car for those hot nights in the city. Sinkers don't perform well until the winds are eighteen to twenty knots or over, and their main function is to ride waves. So unless you can afford a couple of boards, or want to be able to sail on only those few days a year, you'd be wiser to consider buying a longer and more versatile board.

You also need to consider your weight and the type of water surface you'll be sailing on most often. If you are a heavier person, for example, you'll certainly need a board with extra flotation, width, or length. And if you plan to chop jump on a lake as opposed to surf on the ocean, you'll definitely want a more floaty hull shape.

Width

As I said before, board width is an important consideration. It plays a major role in determining how much flotation you have, how soon you can plane, how much wetted surface you have, and how well your board will handle under various conditions. Most importantly, the width of your board's midsection must be carefully matched to its length and to the width of your nose and tail. In board design, symmetry is crucial. This is because a board that is proportionately too wide for its plan shape (i.e., has too narrow a tail and nose for its width) will cause cavitation (loss of grip due to turbulence and air bubbles in the water) when you try to turn it at high speeds. The theory here is that when a board is turning on its edge, the water line can't keep up with the rapid change occurring along the board's rails if the midsection is wide but the tail very narrow. As a result, the fin is forced out of the water, the board cavitates, and the rider loses control.

It is generally accepted that the stronger the winds and the higher the board speeds, the narrower the plan shape must be to inhibit cavitation when turning. So, contrary to what

7.4

many people think, board width and outline rather than board length is the main factor that determines how well a board will handle in heavy air at high speeds or in light air at low speeds. In fact, a very short and narrow board will be as fast if not faster than a longer board on a reach because it has less overall wetted surface. Less wetted surface means less friction and less friction translates into higher potential hull speeds. Proof of this was Fred Haywood's victory at the Weymouth speed trials in 1983. At 210 pounds, Fred went over thirty knots on an eight-foot six-inch board that was only nineteen inches wide (Figure 7.4). Such a board would seldom be used for recreational sailing (since the only way you can turn a board that narrow is in long, drawn out arcs), but if your primary aim is to go fast and straight, reducing wetted surface is where it's at.

The big disadvantage with any narrow hull shape is that because it has less wetted surface and therefore less flotation, it takes considerably more wind to get it moving fast enough to hop up onto a plane. Fred's nineteen-inch-wide board really didn't start to shine until the winds hit thirty to thirty-five knots. This is why you need to consider your weight and the winds you are most likely to be sailing in very carefully. The heavier you are, the more board length and/or width and thickness you'll need to keep the board from submerging in lighter airs; the less wind you have, regardless of your weight, the more board volume you'll need to have sufficient planing surface.

Another disadvantage with a narrow hull shape is that a narrower board is stiffer and less maneuverable at slower speeds, whereas a wider board enables you to turn smoothly around the plan shape and to execute quicker, more pivoty turns, even in light airs. In addition, a wider board will make it easier to jump chop or waves.

At its widest point, a board can be anywhere from eighteen to thirty inches across, but the length-to-width ratio should remain around 4.5:1. So, on a nine-foot board, maintaining this ratio would call for a width of twenty-four inches, or two feet. Boards that have a lower length-to-width ratio (wider boards) are more suited to lighter winds and smaller surf. Boards that have a higher length-to-width ratio (narrower boards) are more suited to heavier winds and larger surf.

Wide Points

The wide point on a board (i.e. the place where it is widest) is an important design consideration. As a general rule, the wide point on a performance board will be anywhere from its middle (Figure 7.5) to six inches forward of the middle. The more forward it is, the wider and smoother the arcs the board will turn in (Figure 7.5A). For high winds and larger waves, the wide point on a board needs to be more forward. This holds the tail in at higher speeds, since the board can carry a less abrupt curve aft and yet still maintain an evenly curved plan shape. The opposite is true with a wide point set aft—you have a more abrupt curve toward the tail, so the board is looser, or "squirrellier," and therefore easier to lose control of at high speeds (Figure 7.5B). In short, wide points are best set forward for heavy air and stiffer turns, and best set aft for lighter air and looser turns.

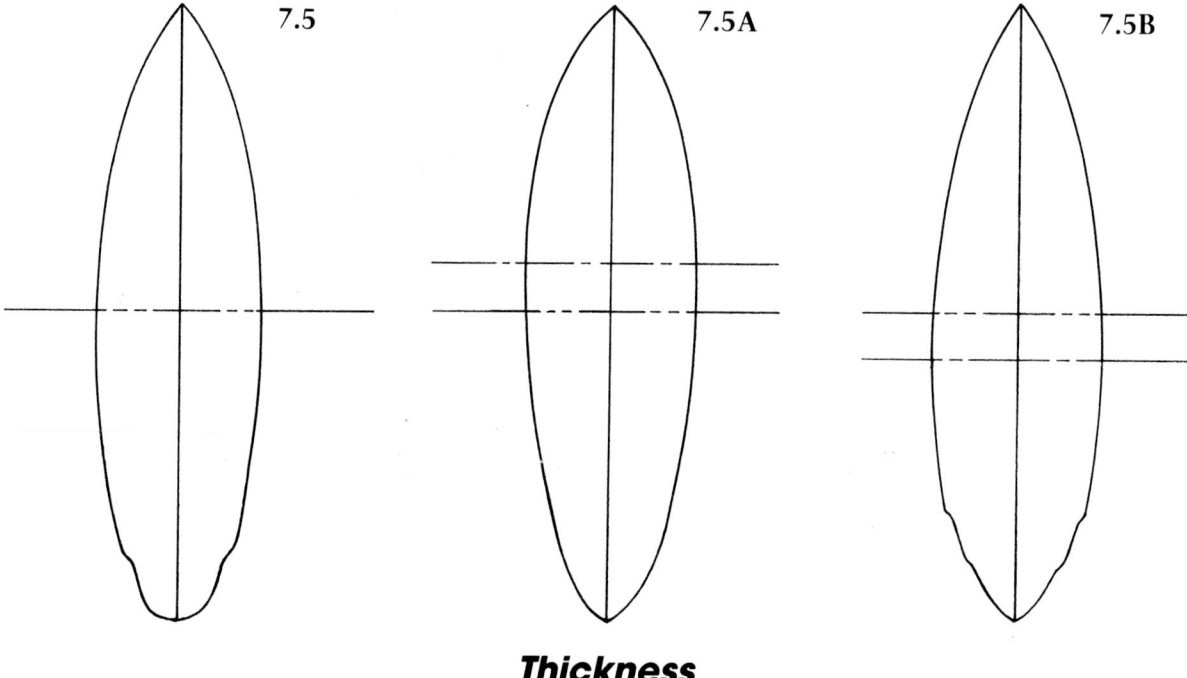

7.5   7.5A   7.5B

Thickness

Another important consideration when choosing a performance board is thickness. What you want to avoid is a board that is too thick for your weight. Boards that are too thick are so buoyant that they place your feet high up off the water. This makes it very difficult to get the board to lean over and slice through the water with its rails for the tight, carving turns that are such fun to make on a short board. But you also want to be careful not to get a board that's too thin. A board that's too thin may not float you well enough or may break in half in surf or when jumping a lot of chop, or the rails may slice the water too deeply during turns.

Like every other aspect of board design, thickness needs to be considered against the backdrop of the entire plan shape. A board designed for high speed, for example, should be considerably thinner than one designed for

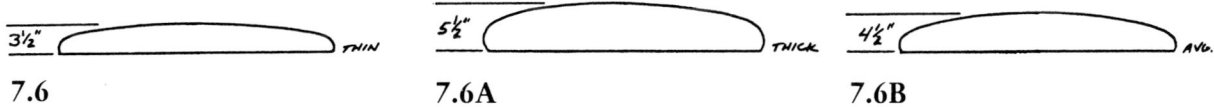

7.6 **7.6A** **7.6B**

light air. As a rule, three and a half inches is about as thin as you want to go (Figure 7.6) and five and a half inches about as thick (Figure 7.6A). For most people, a thickness of around four to four and a half inches is best (Figure 7.6B). In general, though, the heavier the sailor, the thicker you'll need to go; the lighter the sailor, the thinner. This last point can't be stressed enough, because so much of the turning you do on a performance board is off of the rails. If you can't sink the rails at all into a turn, or if they sink too much (like up to your feet when turning), you've gone to the extreme. If your board is too thick and you don't have the weight to sink that rail in when the winds are up and you're flying, you're going to have difficulty turning it. It will want to "bounce out." In light airs, though, when that same board isn't moving as fast, you might do fine on it. And just the opposite can be true. If your board is too thin and sinks when you turn unless it's really blowing, you either need to get a thicker board and rails or lose some weight!

Rails

The rail configuration on a performance board is critical, too. Thin rails that are turned down, or "pinched," are good for high-speed sailing (Figure 7.7). They help prevent "spinning out" because they separate the water easily and provide a sharp edge for holding the board in when planing or making a fast, carving type of jibe. They also slice through chop when going straight at high speed. Rounder rails that are less turned down allow water to creep up over the rail (Figure 7.7A). This helps hold the board on the water and allows for easier turning in lighter winds because the rails are more buoyant. A rail which is very round, however, will not "bite" the water on turns as well as a thinner rail. It will sideslip more and move slower than a thin rail line configuration. A "boxier" rail, which has a less gradual curve and a more visible down edge, is best for lighter airs (Figure 7.7B). It pro-

vides the buoyancy necessary to keep the board gliding through turns even when board speed has dropped, and it has a nice release point for the water to run off—something a rounded rail doesn't provide.

In general, the higher the winds a board is designed for, the thinner and more turned down the rails should be. The lower the winds the board is designed for, the more rounded and / or boxy the rails should be.

With most boards, however the rails are shaped, you should find rails that are harder in the front, softer in the middle, and harder again aft (Figure 7.8). Having less sharp rails in the middle, at the pivot point, prevents "tripping" on the rail when doing turns or maneuvering on waves. Having the rails get hard again aft provides for added bite when turning. But this rail change should not be visible on a well-shaped board. The transi-

7.7 **7.7A** **7.7B**

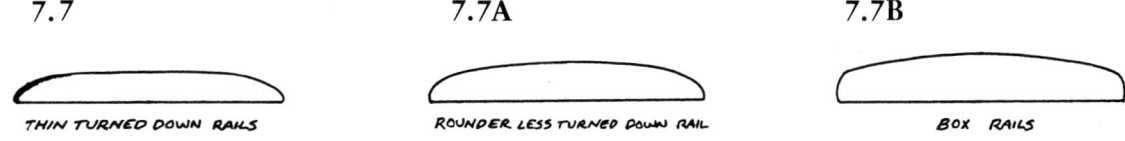

THIN TURNED DOWN RAILS   ROUNDER LESS TURNED DOWN RAIL   BOX RAILS

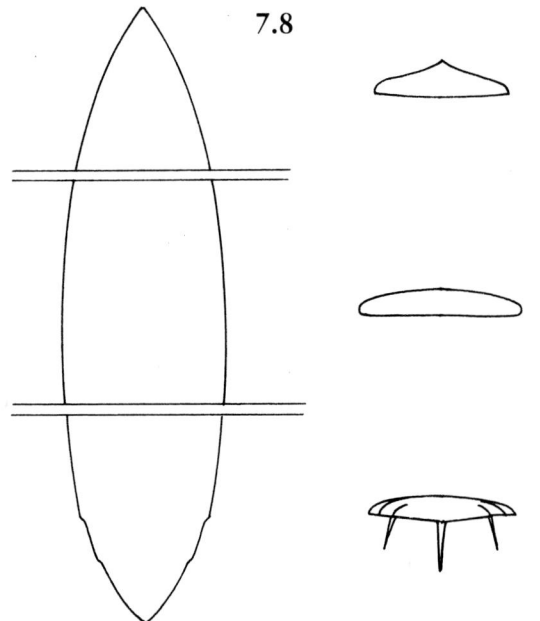

7.8

tions on the rail line should be so smooth and gradual that you won't be able to notice a place on the rails where hard begins and soft ends.

This point about smooth transitions on the rail line applies to the entire board. In fact, veteran sailboard shaper Jimmy Lewis, who has shaped four world speed record boards, believes that you can always tell a well-shaped board from a poorly shaped one by eye alone. In other words, what is pleasing to the eye will be pleasing to the water. No abrupt curves or changes, just flowing lines. No matter what angle you look at a board from, whether from the nose back, the tail forward, midsection across, or diagonally, it should always have pleasing, flowing curves.

Scoop

With shorter boards and narrower tails comes a need for less scoop, or "kick," in the nose of the board. In general, one inch of scoop for every foot of length is a good rule to follow with performance boards. However, if you're surfing steep waves, you may need more scoop (Figure 7.9), whereas if you're not surfing at all, you can use less scoop (Figure 7.9A). Less scoop translates into a little more overall potential board speed. When determining the proper degree of scoop in a board, make sure that it's been shaped into the board gradually, especially where it merges with the flat aft section of the board. If it hasn't been shaped in this manner, the board will either push water or cavitate badly at high speeds.

7.9

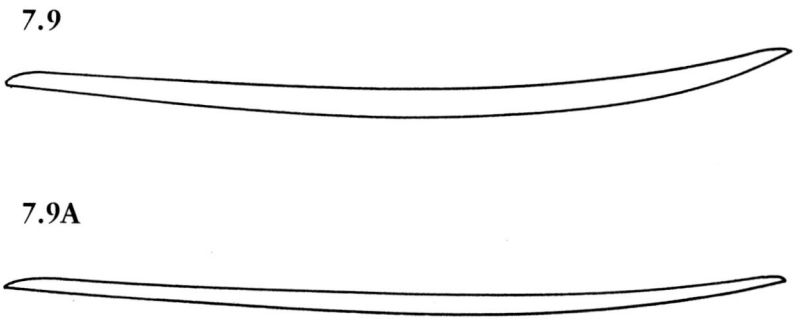

7.9A

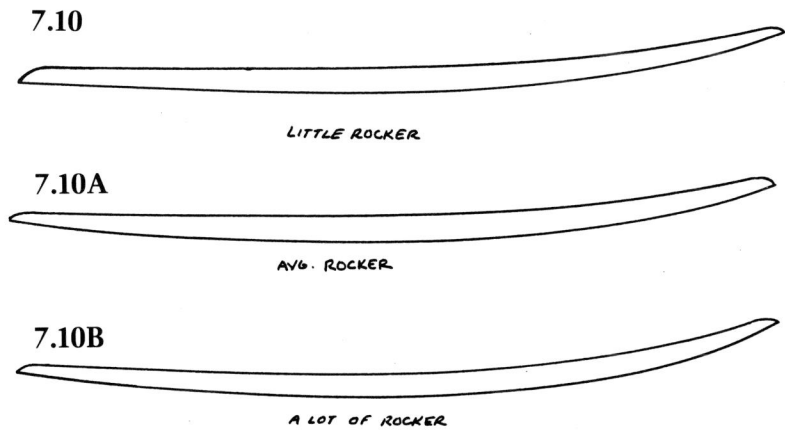

7.10

LITTLE ROCKER

7.10A

AVG. ROCKER

7.10B

A LOT OF ROCKER

Rocker

Rocker or bottom curve is the degree of lift a board has at its nose and tail. A board with less rocker and a flatter bottom is faster overall (Figure 7.10) but is also stiffer in the turns and more difficult to manage in the surf and when jibing. So a board with less rocker is more appropriate for a lake sailor (Figures 7.10–10A), while a surfer will definitely need more rocker (Figure 7.10B). However, all boards need rocker to some degree if they are to turn and jibe with any speed and fluidity.

A dead·flat-tailed board is very fast but extremely difficult to jibe at high speed.

As with everything else, rocker is a matter of compromise. If you put a lot of rocker in a board, it's going to turn incredibly well but move incredibly slowly. And if you put almost no rocker in a board, it's going to move like lightning but turn like a Mack truck. Again, you need to consider the type of sailing you want to do to figure out how much rocker is best for you.

Bottom Shape

Bottom shape refers to the shape of a board's bottom from side to side as opposed to fore to aft. Rounded bottoms are directionally less stable than flat ones and are a little easier to turn when banked (Figure 7.11). Round or V bottoms also help you go faster upwind, especially in chop. However, the most popular bottom shape for performance boards is mostly flat, with a little bit of "V" in the tail to assist in turning and edge control (Figure 7.12). The V makes for easier rail-to-rail transitions when turning, but it also takes a small bit of snap and thrust out of the turn. Despite these drawbacks, however, some V is necessary since a dead-flat bottom on a board can be dif-

ficult to turn because the rail line doesn't have enough curve when you put it on edge. V is sometimes put into the nose of boards, since it's good for upwind sailing because it breaks chop.

ROUNDED DECK

VEE BOTTOM

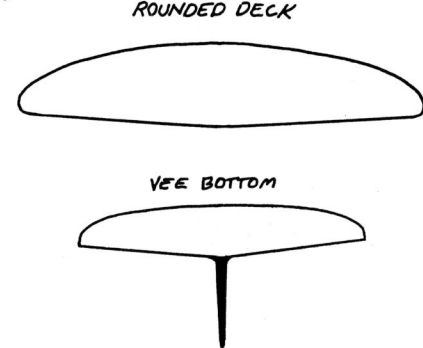

Slalom boards

Perhaps the most extreme version of bottom V is the kind you see on present-day slalom boards. These boards have a heavy, double concave, with a big middle V in the center (Figure 7.13). This V helps to prevent sideslip, serving very much like a daggerboard so the board can still make good headway when sailing upwind. These slalom boards are the hot tip for sailors who need a versatile performance board that can go upwind and yet still carve jibes off the rail.

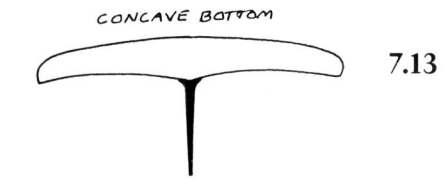

CONCAVE BOTTOM

7.13

Concaves and Channels

Some designers will shape a concave into the belly of a board to help it initiate planes and to reduce water drag at high speeds. Such designs are common in speed trials boards, where speed is more important than the ability to turn radically off the tail (Figure 7.14).

7.14

Some speciality bottoms used on three-finned boards have channeled tail sections (Figure 7.15). Such channels help loosen up the board when turning or jibing by helping to create turbulence under the tail of the board, which in turn creates an air pocket that cuts down on hydrodynamic drag. The air pockets also create lift, which both loosens up the board and makes it easier to get on a plane in marginal wind conditions.

7.15

Nose Shape

The shape of the nose should be widened or narrowed according to the needs of the overall plan shape. So it follows that a wider board has a wider nose (Figure 7.16) and a narrower board has a narrower nose (Figure 7.16A). Reducing nose width stops bouncing and digging in chop and therefore is desirable if you sail frequently in a lot of chop. But a narrower nose does make uphauling, water starting, and tacking a bit more difficult, since there is less flotation up forward. Also, too narrow a nose decreases the initial lift you need for jumping. On the other hand, too wide

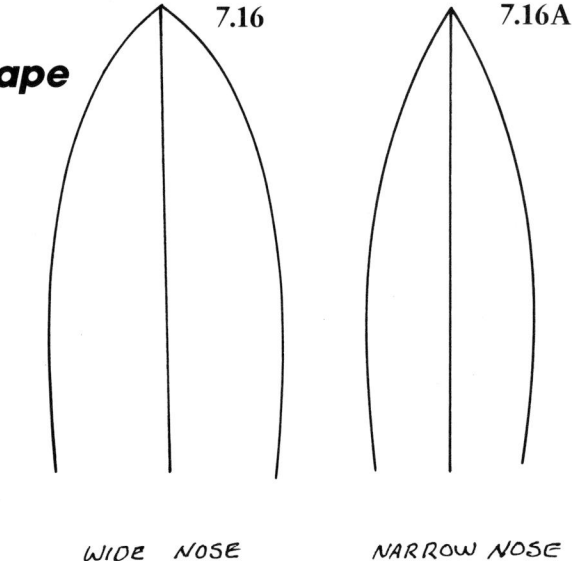

7.16   7.16A

WIDE NOSE   NARROW NOSE (NO NOSE)

a nose is generally undesirable for a performance board; it does make it easier to sail, but only at the expense of inhibiting speed since it will push water unnecessarily in stronger winds.

Tail Shapes

The tail shape you choose for your performance board is fairly critical. It will largely determine how fast you can go, what types of turns you can make (and at what speeds), how high you can jump, and how well you can maneuver in the surf under various types of wind and wave conditions—providing, of course, that the other design factors follow.

In general, a wide-tailed board is more versatile than a narrow-tailed board. A wider tail is better for light airs, beginning sailors, smaller surf, and tighter, short-radius turning, whereas a narrower tail is better for heavy air, advanced sailors, large surf, and long, "drawn out" rail turns.

The major advantage to a wide-tailed board and the characteristic that makes it best for those in need of versatility, is that it will float more weight in less wind than a narrow-tailed board will. This means that it can reach planing speeds more quickly and will allow you to begin jumping chop and sailing out through the surf sooner than on a narrower-tailed board.

The major drawbacks with a wide tail (and hence the major advantages of a narrow tail) don't begin to surface until either the waves are big or the winds are very strong. If winds are strong, a wide tail will cavitate far sooner than a narrow tail, as well as have a nasty habit of "spinning out" when you attempt a powerful, carving jibe off the rail line. The reason for this is that when a wide tail is put on its edge, it wants to "plane out," which is what happens when, because the fin is farther from the rail on wider-tailed boards, it tends to leave the water and permit the tail to skid. If the waves are big, additional problems arise. During a bottom turn in big waves, for example, a wide-tailed board that is too buoyant won't allow you to dig the rail in enough and still keep the fin in to prevent a spinout when you carve a turn at the bottom of a wave going full speed.

The best way to determine whether or not your tail is too wide for the winds or waves you're in (or in some instances, if you've got too *much* fin area in the water) is to try turning your board. If you feel that you're "bouncing out" on your turns, it usually means that your tail is too wide for your weight. That same board in the same conditions might work well for someone heavier (or, given lighter conditions, it might work for you), but unless you can dig in that tail, it's not the right board for that wind speed. Sometimes a smaller fin can correct this problem (see below).

As you can see, tail shape is like every other aspect of board design. You must keep in mind your weight and the kind of winds you'll be sailing in. The more wind and the faster you go, the thinner your rails and the narrower your overall plan shape and tail must be. The slower you go, the thicker your rails and the wider your plan shape and tail must be. How thick or how thin, how wide or how narrow, this depends on your weight and how much pressure you can apply on the tail to turn the board. At 130 pounds, the boards I ride in twenty knots are a whole lot thinner than the ones my heavier friends like Fred Haywood and Matt Schweitzer ride. If I get on one of Matt's heavy-air, tri-fin boards in a decent blow, for example, I can't keep the fins in the water. Each time I try to turn, I just bounce out of the water or sideslip out of control. If Matt gets on one of my boards he sinks the rails and the board digs and becomes unresponsive.

Pin Tail

If you plan to sail in a lot of wind or in large surf, chances are you'll need a pin tail or rounded pin-tail tail shape (Figure 7.17). The pin tail is the ultimate high-speed performance board. The advantages of the pin tail are that it carves powerful, drawn out turns at high speeds, it remains in control even when reaching full speed at thirty-five knots plus or when dropping down the face of an eight-foot wave, and it's the fastest tail shape you can use for a performance board. In addition, narrow tails are much less likely to cavitate than wider tails.

Most pin tails are set up with a single-fin arrangement and are slightly longer for a given weight of rider. The big disadvantage with this is that your board is not altogether versatile. For example, a single-finned pin tail is stiff in turning unless the winds or waves are up, and landing one after a jump is more difficult. With just one fin in the water, the board is hard to control when you land unless you do it perfectly. Another drawback with the single-finned pin tail is that while it does the best bottom turns when surfing, it doesn't come off the top of a wave as easily when you lose speed; unlike a three-finned thruster, it doesn't have a natural tendency to glide around sharply on its own.

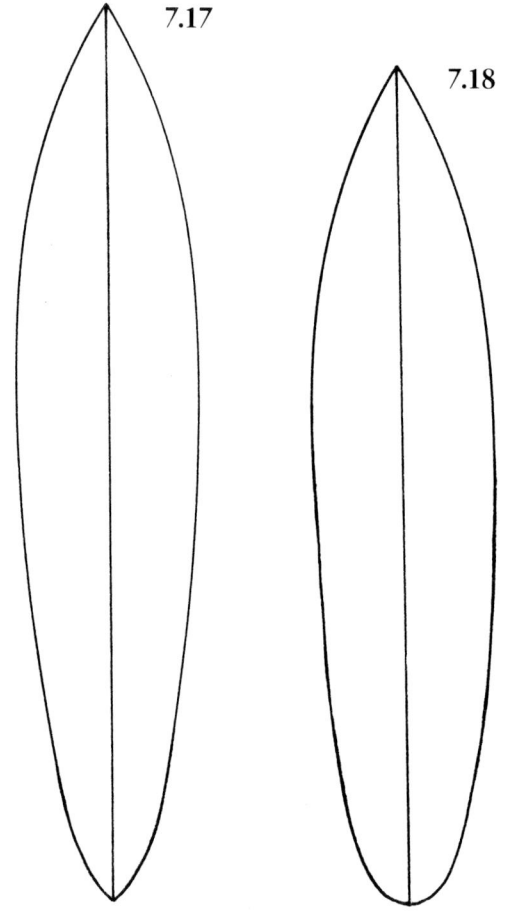

7.17

7.18

Round Tail

A round tail is simply a wider pin tail and, due to its versatility, is a good tail to have on most performance boards (Figure 7.18). When your board is set up with removable fin boxes, you can sail a round tail either as a thruster with three fins or as a single fin.

The advantages of the wider, round-tail setup with three fins are that it is controllable at high speeds, it turns very smoothly and loosely, it can handle medium-sized surf, and it will work adequately in stronger winds. The narrower the round tail, the better it will perform in higher winds and larger surf; the wider the round tail, the better it will perform in lower winds and smaller surf. (Actually, this width–ratio theory is true with any tail shape.)

The only time a round tail is totally inappropriate is in very high winds or big surf. Under such conditions, you'll reach speeds that are too great for the width of the tail and end up going out of control (again, too much speed for the width).

Square or Squash Tail

Square and squash tails are great for any-body who wants to ride the shortest possible board for their weight (Figure 7.19). Such tails turn easily in a pivoting style, jump easily, plane quickly, and work well in light-to-medium air for heavy riders who need extra flotation. These are also fine tail shapes for lake sailors and chop jumpers who sail in light airs or for surfers who seldom ride big waves, especially if they're set up as a thruster.

Swallow Tail

The swallow tail allows for a wider tail configuration by not requiring the tail to taper in as far toward the board's center (Figure 7.20). Most swallow tails are simply square-tails with a swallow cut into them, and they sail in just about the same way. The only difference is that when on edge, the swallow tail acts like a pin tail because one side of the swallow is out of the water and one side is really digging into it. The advantage this type of board holds over a pin tail or round tail is that its slightly wider tail helps keep it loose in light air and helps heavier riders remain on a plane. Swallow tails are also very nice looking compared with a square tail.

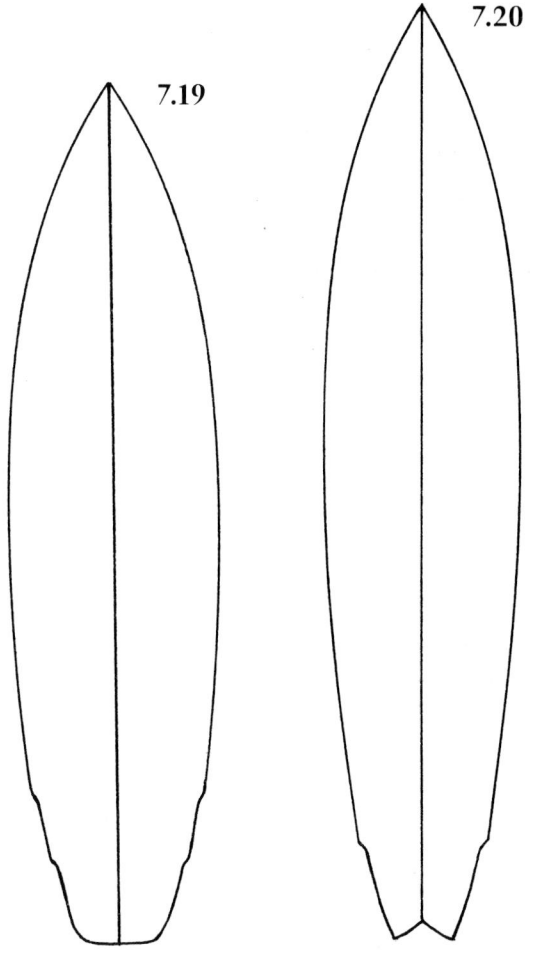

7.19

7.20

Asymmetrical Boards and Can Openers

Asymmetrical boards, or boards with uneven rails and tail sections (can openers) (Figure 7.21), are only for wave riders. Such boards, though not seen much, have been around in the surfing world for a long time because surfers have long known that the best board for doing a bottom turn is a narrow out-line with the wide point set forward, while the best board for coming back down off the top of a wave is a wider outline with the wide point set aft. For this reason, an asymmetri-cal board is actually two boards in one. A nar-row longer board on the bottom turn and a

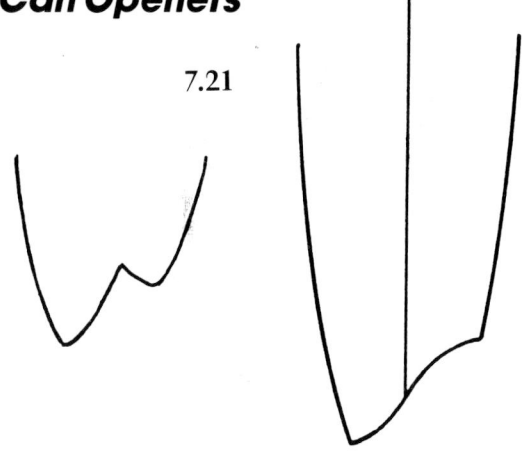

7.21

wider shorter board for coming off the top. In this way, surfers have a board that gives them good bite for the fast bottom turn and a tail that gives them extra flotation, glide, and snap power for the slower top turn or cutback.

Sailboarders have picked up on this surfer's knowledge recently, and a lot of people are experimenting with asymmetrical tails. Craig Masonville was the first to start experimenting seriously with them on windsurfers. The big problem with such a tail is that it's totally unversatile. If you have one made, you can only surf well in one direction and only on one particular type of wave. In other words, this is a speciality board that only more advanced wave riders are likely to need or want, as one of several in their "quiver."

Wingers

Wingers, just like the swallow tail, are far from a gimmick. Concaved wings both add to rail bite for turning and help prevent cavitation (Figure 7.22). They do so, though, at the expense of looser turning, since they decrease tail rocker by bringing the rails of the board closer to the water, causing a flatter and stiffer tail.

Wings that are not concaved serve a different function: they enable you to have a narrower tail without too narrow a board or too abrupt a curve in the after section of the plan shape (Figures 7.19–20). This means that you can keep more foam under your feet and yet still have a narrow and more responsive tail. It also means that nonconcaved wings will provide for a looser board but won't in any way help to prevent cavitation. Sometimes, two or even three sets of wings will be added to a board to help pull in the tail dimensions.

7.22

Fins

Fins play a very important role in determining how well a board will perform for a sailor of a given weight in a given wind condition. As a general rule, the larger the fin area, the greater your lateral resistance, the better your directional stability, the greater the lift when turning, the better your pointing ability, and the greater your drag. The converse is true with smaller fin area. But this is where the usefulness of rules breaks down.

Choosing proper fin size, especially in heavy air, is sort of a Catch-22 affair. Three problems are involved: cavitation; spinning out; or bouncing out. Cavitation occurs when you're traveling fast on a straight reach or beginning a turn and your fin, or skeg, loses contact with the water, causing an air pocket to form along its side. The resulting loss of lateral resistance makes the board slide sideways. You can help this situation by either increasing your fin area or foiling your fin, depending on whether your fin is too small or improperly foiled.

Spinning out occurs when you bank very sharply while turning and your fin pops out of the water, allowing your tail to slide. The only way to deal with this is to increase your fin area or add thrusters, get a better-foiled fin, or turn less sharply. The thrusters or side fins help the most, though.

Bouncing out occurs when either your tail is too wide or your skeg is too large for your weight—when you get going too fast, you just bounce out of the water. Using a narrower-tailed board, decreasing your fin area, or eliminating or decreasing thruster fins will help this situation, although a fin that is too large for your weight and causes bouncing out in heavier airs might work fine in lighter airs. It is similar to sailing in high winds on a standard board with the daggerboard down; the board wants to rail-ride because the daggerboard wants to plane up and onto the surface. The same is true with too large a fin or thrusters.

The best way to find the right fins for your board is to consider the three W's, especially your weight, and to experiment on the water with different fins before you decide you don't like your board. As you experiment, keep the following things in mind:

1. Heavier riders can handle larger fins, since they can exert more force on the tail to keep the fin from popping out.

2. If you can't hold the fin in when turning, you need to go to a smaller fin.

3. Since heavier winds and more board speed tends to increase fin cavitation problems, it generally holds that you need smaller fins for heavy air and very high speeds.

However, the ultimate goal is to find a fin that's both controllable in turns and can handle high speeds, whatever its size or shape.

Fin Position

If your board has an adjustable fin box, moving your fin(s) will also change the way your board turns. Moving your fin(s) forward will loosen up your board and make it easier to turn in short, tight arcs, whereas moving your fin(s) aft will stiffen up your board and make for wider-arced turns.

As a rule of thumb, you move your fin(s) aft to increase control and to help your board go straight, and you move your fin(s) forward for light air and small waves to increase

maneuverability. With thruster fins, moving them closer together will make a board snappier, while spreading them apart will, to a certain extent, make a board more "tracky" and drawn out.

Fin Rake

The rake of a fin will also change board control. The more rake a fin has, i.e., the more swept back it is, the better it will hold you in the water and the longer and more drawn out your turns will be (Figure 7.23). With a more vertical fin, on the other hand, you can make sharper, more pivotal turns (Figure 7.23A). The straight vertical fin used in slalom and course racing has a tendency to hold the board in well when sailing in a straight line but is quite difficult to control when turning at high speed (Figure 7.23B). On the whole, a compromise shape is the best, but at one time or another your needs may require either a more vertical or more rakey fin shape.

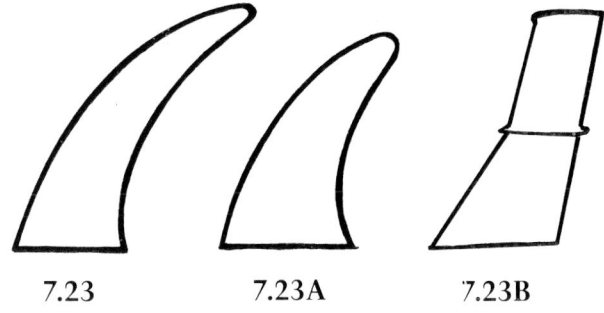

7.23   7.23A   7.23B

Fin Types

The common fin you'll usually see on performance boards has its maximum point of fullness about a third back from its front and has a nice smooth taper from front to back. In appearance, it looks a lot like a shark's fin, having a pretty gradual curve from base to tip. Personally, this is the fin shape that I like (Figure 7.23A).

One very popular fin is called a fence fin (Figure 7.24). The fence fin looks very much like the standard fin. It differs only in that it

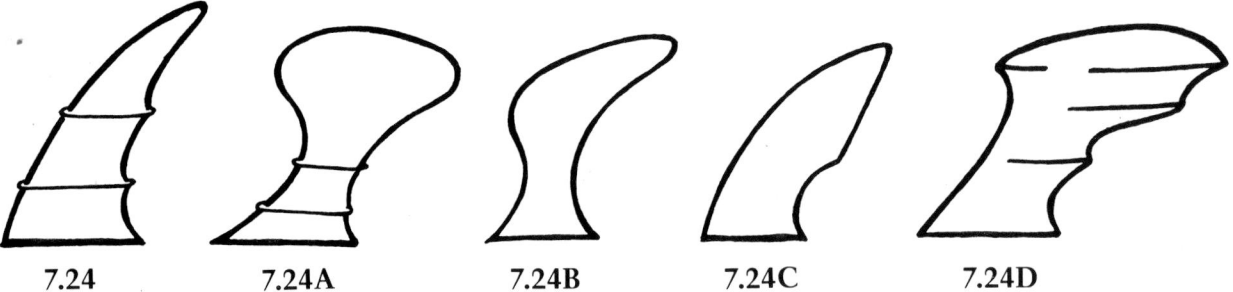

7.24   7.24A   7.24B   7.24C   7.24D

has two to three fences placed on its side in a horizontal plane. The purpose of fences is to prevent cavitation at high speeds. Cavitation starts at the base of the fin and then rolls down toward the fin tip, creating an ever increasing pocket of air as it moves along the fin. The fences serve to stop this from happening by braking the flow of cavitation starting from the first fence, which is positioned just up from the base.

In the past few years, "football" fins have become popular. These fins have a very narrow base and a wide tip (Figure 7.24A). The theory behind these fins is that by having the tip in front of the base, the flow of cavitation can't get out to the end of the fin. In this way, the football fin helps the rider maintain control at high speeds when cavitation becomes a problem. I suspect that over the next few years we will be seeing a lot of development with fins such as these.

The foot fin operates on the same principle as the football fin but is just a less extreme version, having a less pronounced, or bulbous tip (Figure 7.24B).

Another popular fin development is taking a standard-shaped fin and foil and cutting out the base in the aft section, leaving the overall profile of the fin the same. In this way, turning isn't inhibited by extra fin area down low, and cavitation is reduced at the base (Figure 7.24C). Still another fin seeks to combine the qualities of both the fence fin and the football fin in one called "strata fin", these are good for high speeds on thruster setups (Figure 7.24D).

New fin shapes are coming out on a daily basis. During the next several years you can expect to see a number of new designs. Some will be good, some not so good. My suggestion is to let someone else do the research and design before you go spending your money on "the hottest fin since windsurfing began!" In other words, watch out for gimmicks.

Fin Foil

Fin foil (the cross-sectional configuration) is just as important as fin shape. An improperly foiled fin will always have a negative impact on performance. In the past, when good plastic fins were hard to come buy, the ideal fins were hand-shaped from glass. Today, though, the best fins are made from plastic because they are made from the mold of a perfectly shaped fin. It just takes too much time to shape a perfectly foiled fiberglass fin for each board. But a drawback with plastic is that it's generally more flexible or brittle than glass.

In most instances, the best foil retains the one-third draft profile with a fairly thick foil that tapers evenly in smooth curves all the way from the front to the back (Figure 7.25),

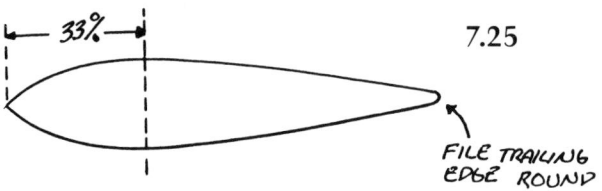

7.25

FILE TRAILING EDGE ROUND

FULLY FOILED CROSS SECTION

the front being pretty rounded and the back being pretty sharp, although not razor sharp. And this is not for safety's sake alone. Too fine an edge brings the water together too fast at the back so that the water particles collide and then create air bubbles. So the best back edge has a very slight flat edge running from the base to the tip. As far as overall thickness is concerned, a thinner foil is better for higher speeds and a thicker foil is better for lower speeds.

Thrusters

For the most part, the above facts and tips apply to three-fin setups, also known as a "thruster."

Perhaps the nicest thing about a thruster is its versatility. For example, you can sail it as a single fin in heavy airs by mounting a larger fin in the center and removing the rail fins; you can sail it with the two rail fins with a larger center fin; or you can sail it with all three fins the same size (a true thruster). The important thing to bear in mind when experimenting with these options is this: you want to have the loosest possible board and still ensure maximum control and minimum cavitation.

As far as wide tails go, three fins are nice, since they allow you to have width and yet enable you to prevent spinning out in the turns. They also help inhibit cavitation, with one disadvantage. Unlike a cavitated single fin, you can't "reset" a three-finner unless you come off a plane. This means dropping speed, setting the fins, and getting on a plane again.

One big advantage with a thruster is that it allows you to regain control after a jump far more quickly than a single fin does. This is because as soon as you land, one of its fins will immediately come into contact with the water, thereby reestablishing control. Another thing that's neat about thrusters is that they tend to glide easily through turns, even when you lose a bit of speed. Single fins won't do this—if you don't maintain proper pressure on the rail or the winds drop as you're turning, the rail is likely to sink and the board will stop turning and also sink.

Summary

Now that you have a basic understanding of performance board design principles, you're probably somewhat confused as to what to do with all this information. This is only natural, for the things to consider and balance are many. My intention in overloading this chapter with information was not to encourage you to go out and design your own custom board. In fact, my advice is to leave the designing to the experts. Where these facts will be most useful to you is in eliminating and correcting problems that arise when actually sailing your performance board or when it comes time to go out and buy a new one. Refer back to this chapter from time to time—the more you sail, the more likely you'll be to grasp the facts and theories I've discussed.

Perhaps the best way to go about choosing your board is to make notes on each section in this chapter, trying to determine which design features are best suited to your needs. By starting with length and working through to fin design, you should be able to eliminate a number of possibilities and arrive at a general design that feels right for you. Remember, though, that any design you choose won't do everything well. Compromises will have to be made, and it's a good idea to keep this in mind as you begin your quest for your "ideal" sailboard.

After you've chosen a general design and dimensions, you should talk with your friends and other sailors at your local sailing spot to see if they think you're on the right track. When you are confident in your plan, then start shopping for a board or talking to the shapers who will make you one. If a plastic board is what you want, you probably won't be able to meet your exact specifications; however, you should be able to find a good compromise because there are a number of great plastic boards on the market with many designs to choose from. Having learned the basic design principles, you'll also be able to avoid buying a "lemon." By keeping an eye out for smooth flowing lines and by checking length-to-width ratios, thicknesses, rail shapes, rocker, etc., you'll be able to sort out the good production models from the bad.

If you're going for a custom board, at least you'll have the facts you need to discuss the type of board you want and your reasons for wanting it intelligently with your shaper, or shop owner. Starting with your general plan, the two of you should be able to come up with a design that will suit your needs best.

Take your time, ask a lot of questions, and buy your board only after you're totally convinced you've found (or are going to have shaped) the best possible board for your needs. And if you make a mistake, well, try again. You can probably count on buying or trying more than one board before your windsurfing career is over. Personally, I go through dozens a year. But it's a constant learning process.

8. Sails and Other Gear

Over the past five years, performance board sail and equipment theory has changed dramatically several times. Every few months, some radical new development arises which forces us to reconsider many of our once unquestioned assumptions. As I write this very chapter, in fact, some new and exciting changes are underway, particularly in the field of sail design (some of which I'll tell you about shortly). Sail designs will continue to progress, I'm sure, and a lot has been learned up to this point. In this chapter I'll explain the basics about sails and what their different functions are relating to their designs. I'll also go over masts, universals, and other gear and what to look for when purchasing equipment.

Apparent Wind and Sail Design

Since performance boards sail under the influence of apparent wind, understanding apparent wind is essential if you're to grasp the principles of performance sail design and the best ways to handle and tune your sail.

Apparent wind is the combination of true wind (the wind you feel on your face when standing motionless on a beach) and the wind generated by your board's forward speed. The faster you go, the more apparent wind you'll generate and the farther forward of your beam the wind will appear to blow (Figure 8.1). This helps to explain why sailboards can sail "faster than the wind" and why you want to trim your sails in tight, even when sailing with the true wind on the beam. You get going so fast that the apparent wind swings far forward of your beam. This also is why you must often trim your sail as though you're beam reaching when in reality you're on a broad reach. The degree to which apparent wind can affect you, though, is mainly determined by the strength of the wind and the speed at which you're traveling over the water. Larger waves move faster than smaller ones, leading to greater speed and therefore more apparent wind. In short, the heavier the wind and/or the bigger the waves, the more apparent wind you'll generate.

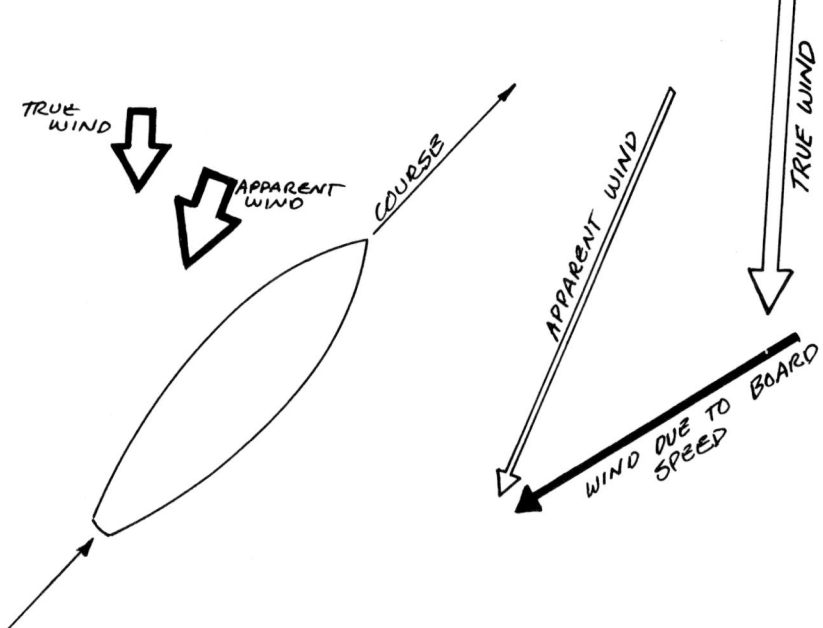

Most big, single-hulled sailboats generate much less apparent wind than a performance board does. For this reason, they carry sails that are very full and that have their points of maximum draft (curve or fullness) set near the middle of the sail. A fuller sail with an aft pocket is good for doing two things: generating lots of lift (which helps a heavy boat point high into the wind) and generating lots of power (Figure 8.2). However, a performance board really doesn't need either of these things in excess. In fact, such a sail would keep your board from ever reaching maximum speed—as soon as the apparent wind started building, the air wouldn't be able to flow across the full curve of the sail fast enough and the sail would begin to flutter or luff. This is why performance sails are cut relatively flat in comparison to big-boat sails and are closer in appearance to catamaran sails: when you're tearing along on a reach or dropping down a wave, you'll generate so much apparent wind that the only way to prevent luffing and going out of control is to have the most efficient sail shape possible. Note that I said "efficient sail shape" as opposed to "flattest sail shape." For it is important to remember that, while

it's nice to have a flat sail when you're dropping down the face of a wave or tearing along on a beam reach, you've still got to have a sail that will give you the power necessary to jump chop, punch out through the surf, or cut back on the face of a wave when you start to lose speed by getting too far away from the curl. In other words, a board-flat sail is never entirely desirable.

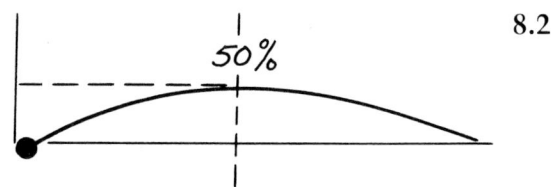

8.2

FULL SAIL WITH 50% DRAFT

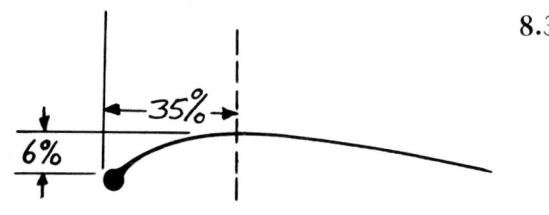

8.3

PERFORMANCE SAIL w/ 35% DRAFT

As a general rule, a properly cut performance sail will have its draft positioned about 35 percent aft of the mast and have a fullness anywhere between 6 percent and 10 percent (Figure 8.3). Within this range of fullness, the most speed will be generated for the given amount of sailcloth. Those who sail most often in moderate airs will carry slightly more curve in their sails and want their pockets to rest more aft, while those who sail most often in heavy air or in the surf will want their sails cut flatter and their pockets to remain more forward.

Performance sails are wider at the top and narrower at the bottom than standard sailboard sails. This type of tall, narrow sail (often called a high-aspect ratio sail plan) is essential for performance boards, since the shortened foot and boom keep the clew out of the water when making radical turns or riding up and down the face of a wave.

The problem with these higher-aspect ratio sails with larger roaches is that they increase mast bend and heel at the expense of overall speed. This is why performance sailors who seldom surf normally choose a sail that is wider at the bottom and shorter along the luff. Such a sail provides more speed due to a shorter and stiffer mast and longer boom, yet (provided it's not too long at the foot) still allows for the radical, carving type jibes that performance boards are famous for. An exception to this rule is the newly developed RAF, or rotating asymmetrical foil, which is cut and designed with less luff curve and a clean foil making it just as fast if not faster than low aspect sails in planing conditions (explained shortly).

For pure surfing, on the other hand, where your sail can come into contact with the wave face pretty easily, the best sail is one that has the shortest boom and the most efficient shape. A sail, in other words, that gives you all the power you need to fly out through the surf, but one that doesn't overpower you when you're riding back in and trying to carve up

the face of the wave as close to the curl as possible.

Sailcloth

There are two basic types of sailcloth currently being used in performance sail construction: dacron and mylar.

Dacron is a woven cloth that's treated with a resin coating. The size of the thread and the amount of resin used in the coating determine both how resistant it is to stretch and how much it weighs. At present, most dacron-made performance sails are constructed with 3.8-ounce cloth and heavily reinforced at points of stretch and wear.

The big disadvantage with dacron is that, in order to get a sail that's resistant to stretch (i.e. one that can handle tremendous speeds), you have to use a pretty heavy cloth. Unfortunately, in performance sailing, where everything is already very light, every ounce of excess weight has a negative impact upon performance. This is why mylar and mylar-like sails are becoming increasingly popular with serious high-performance sailors.

Mylar is a plastic-rolled film that's extraordinarily strong and stretch-resistant for its weight (25 percent lighter than dacron). But mylar has its disadvantages, too. For example, it needs to be treated with far more care than dacron. Because it's made with stiffer and more brittle glues, you can't just crumple it up or fold it and then stuff it in the trunk of your car and expect it to last. In addition, mylar tears rather easily and is more expensive than dacron. Mylar's tendency to tear can be counteracted by laminating a lightweight dacron layer over one side of the mylar sail. In recent months, mylar sails have also been made with what is called "scrim laminate." This is a polyester fiber which is sandwiched between layers of mylar, leading to a very light, stiff, and tear-resistant sail.

Because it's lighter and more stretch-resistant than dacron, all in all, a mylar sail coated with a light layer of dacron or constructed with scrim laminate is the way to go if maximum performance is your goal.

A word of caution: Wait until a new sail design (or sail construction method) has been thoroughly tested and proven worthy by professionals before you purchase it from your local sailmaker.

Panel Layout

Until very recently, most performance sails were laid out using what is called the "cross-cut" method of construction (Figure 8.4). When this method is used, the panels of the sail are set up perpendicular to the leech and run into the luff at about a forty-five-degree angle. With the development of stiffer masts, many sailmakers are using a new "vertical" method of construction (Figure 8.5). Here, the cloth is laid parallel to the leech with the fabric running into the luff at a slight angle or aligned along both the leech and luff. This method is good for performance sails because it provides for a stiffer leech, which is absolutely necessary for the type of short-luffed, wide-roached sails used on performance boards.

Another advantage with the vertical method is that it's a little stronger than the cross-cut

method. There are fewer seams to chafe and fewer places where the seams intersect the leech. Both these factors are important when using mylar, because although it's less likely to stretch than dacron, it's more likely to tear.

To date, many fine performance sails have been constructed using both the cross-cut and vertical methods. Choosing between them is really a matter of personal preference, as is the type of cloth you want in your sail.

Sail Construction

More than other sailors, performance sailors need a sail that can withstand a lot of high wind and abuse from wipeouts and extreme water pressure from waves. By looking for a few special features when purchasing a sail, you can normally assure yourself that you'll get what you need.

The first thing to inspect is the stitching. It should be smooth and even, and there should be no visible creases, puckers, or pulled spots along any of the seams. And all major seams should be double-stitched if intended for use in heavy surf.

The second thing to look for is a well-sewn mast sock and proper reinforcement at major wear spots (head, tack, clew, and boom cuta-

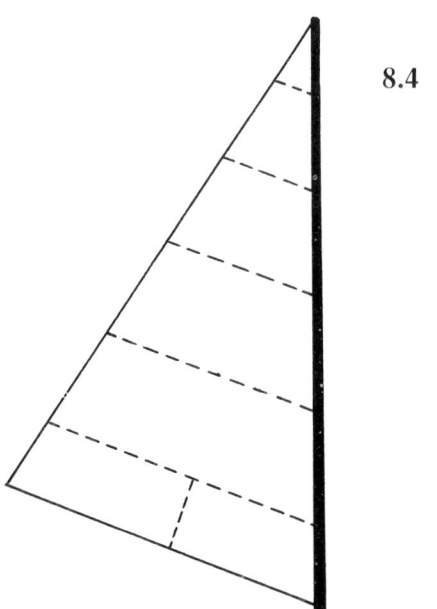

8.4

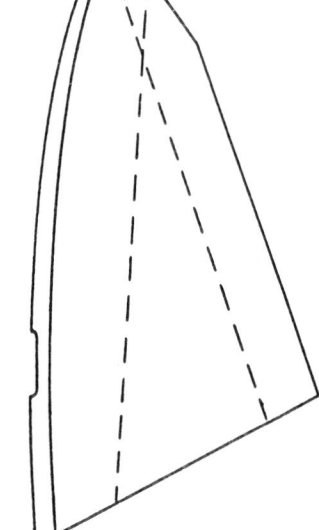

8.5

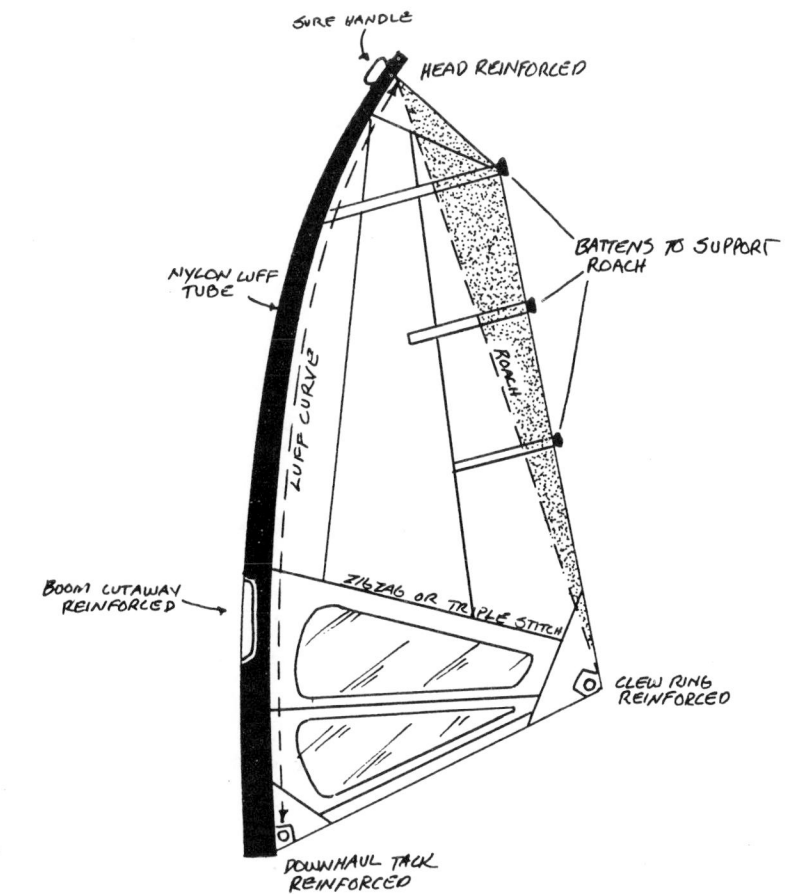

SURE HANDLE

HEAD REINFORCED

BATTENS TO SUPPORT ROACH

NYLON LUFF TUBE

LUFF CURVE

ROACH

BOOM CUTAWAY REINFORCED

ZIGZAG OR TRIPLE STITCH

CLEW RING REINFORCED

8.6

DOWNHAUL TACK REINFORCED

way). If a sail has plenty of extra patches at its three corners and nylon webbing wherever chafing is likely to occur, chances are that it's built to last.(Figure 8.6).

The third thing to consider is the grommets at the head, tack, and clew. All of these should be examined carefully to make certain that they're well mounted and properly reinforced, preferably with nylon webbing.

As you might expect in a market as big as windsurfing, quality is sometimes sacrificed in order to boost production. Perhaps the best way to avoid getting a poor sail, then, is to stick with a brand that's known for its quality and has a reputation to protect. In most instances, a reputable manufacturer will guarantee what he sells and stand behind his product.

Sail Types

Generally, performance sails range in size from thirty-five square feet to sixty-five square feet, although there are some larger sails available for very light winds or extra heavy riders and smaller ones for extremely high winds or children.

The earliest performance sails were known as "pinheads," owing to the narrow, high-aspect roach at the top of the sail (Figure 8.7). In time, however, sailmakers began cutting less and less roach off the top and making shorter-luffed, lower-aspect sail plans, called "fatheads" (Figure 8.7A). For most riders, extreme versions of either of these designs are unnecessary. The best sail for overall use is somewhere between a fathead and a pinhead.

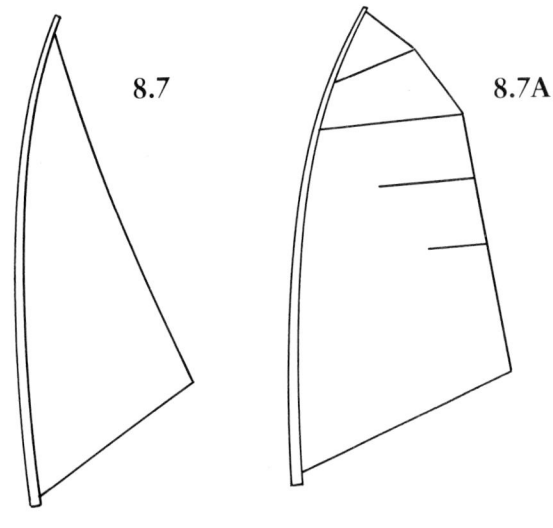

8.7   8.7A

PINHEAD SAIL   FATHEAD SAIL

Currently, most of those being cut are like this, such as most of the sails pictured in this book.

As I pointed out earlier, the most important consideration in choosing a sail is its clew height, since a clew that is too low will inhibit your turning, and a clew that is too high will inhibit obtaining maximum board speed. Surfers generally need higher clews, whereas nonsurfing chop jumpers, racers, and day-sailing hotdoggers do best with lower clews. In racing, the longer-clewed sail is needed not only for more powerful reaching but for going upwind, since such a sail provides for far greater draft control.

Soft Sails

The soft sail is a nonfully battened sail which has one or two full-length battens near the top to hold the leech in shape and a few smaller leech battens which don't run full-length set along the leech. The advantage with a soft sail is that you can read a luff on one very easily, which is important when doing tricks where you need to adjust power in an instant. Soft sails are also lighter and easier to handle than fully battened sails and can be cut in either a high- or low-aspect ratio style. The only major drawbacks with soft sails is that they get blown out faster than fully

battened sails and it's difficult to keep the draft forward in them, making them a less ideal sail for overall speed.

Fully Battened Sails

Fully battened sails are mainly for surf sailors. They provide for a stiffer leech up top, shorter foots, longer luffs, and bigger roaches, leading to a sail with a much shorter boom (Figure 8.8). The advantage, of course, is that your sail drags in the water a lot less when carving a turn on the face of a wave—a distinct advantage. But while the shorter booms and larger heads do make turning a bit easier, these sails are less powerful overall. As a result, fully battened sails are really only popular with a few serious surfers. The majority of sailors, surfers or otherwise, still prefer to use a soft sail.

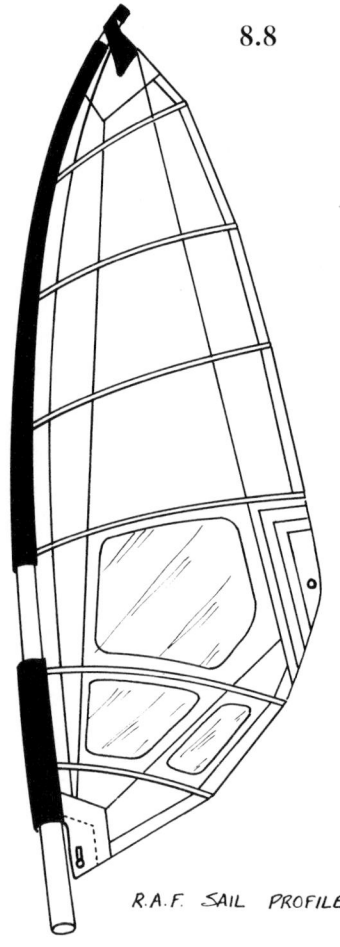

8.8

R.A.F. SAIL PROFILE

Battens

The latest battens for fully battened sails are tapered and absolutely essential for a finely tuned sail; without them, it would be very difficult to create the proper foil. With tapered battens, it's possible to have a nice smooth curve all the way to the 35 percent point in the sail and then have a stiff after section, all the way to the leech. Tapered battens also help to hold this shape in heavy airs, since the after sections of the battens are thick and stiff, preventing the draft from shifting aft of the 35 percent point. The strongest battens are made of glass and epoxy combinations.

Rotating Sails

A recent development in performance board mast construction is the "wing mast," such as the one Fred Haywood used to capture the world speed trials in Weymouth, England. These masts are perfectly straight, extremely stiff, and shaped like an airplane wing. As a result, the wing mast is considerably wider than a standard mast, providing for less aft and little lateral mast bend and, more importantly, for a far better airfoil. If you look at a conventional mast with a sail rigged to it, you will note that there is a "hollow spot" between the mast and the pocket of the sail. The wind is unable to hug this hollow spot, as wind tunnel tests have so often shown (Figure 8.9). As a result, the wind gets slowed down dramatically as it tries to pass from the mast to the pocket on the leeward side of the sail. With a wing mast, the hollow spot is filled, or greatly reduced in depth, and this enables the wind to pass across the sail much faster.

The problem with the wing mast is that it's not a very practical recreational sail. Not only is it a rather fragile rig, but it is also much heavier and more expensive. For this reason, a number of sailmakers have long recognized that any sail and mast which could be designed to create a wing without extra weight and expense would be the ideal setup for performance sailing. In recent months, Barry Spanier and Geoff Borne of Maui Sails have been working on just such a sail and rig, called an "asymmetrical rotating foil" (Fig. 8.10). Basically, what Barry is creating, and what we have been testing, is a fully battened sail that rotates on the mast from side to side. When changing tacks, the leading edge of the sail always has a nice smooth entry on the leeward side, and the draft is held very far forward by the battens, thereby enabling the wind to pass over the back of the sail more swiftly and to reduce pressure on the windward side. Result: a more efficient sail. The advantage of this sail is that it enables one to carry less square footage and get the same amount of power as from a larger sail. In fact, since these sails are about 20 per-

8.9
8.10

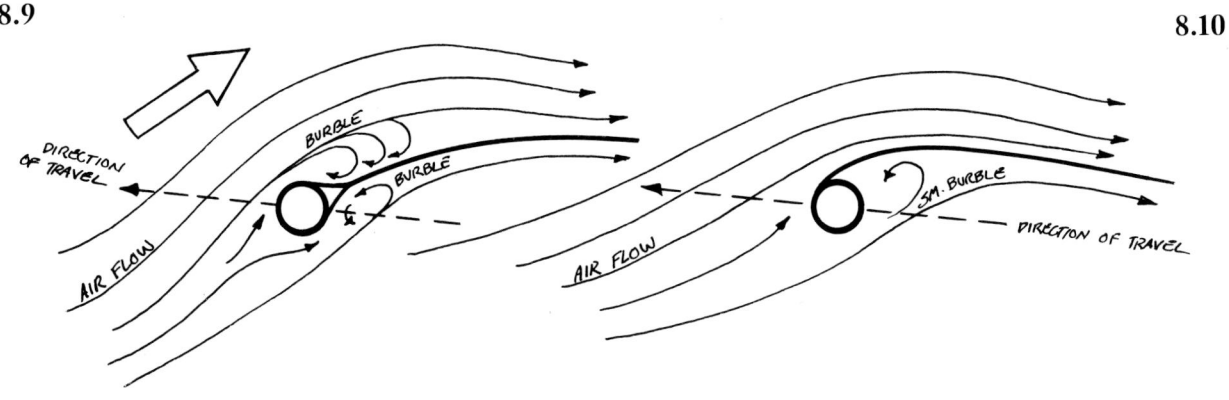

TRADITIONAL SAIL PROFILE

RAF PROFILE

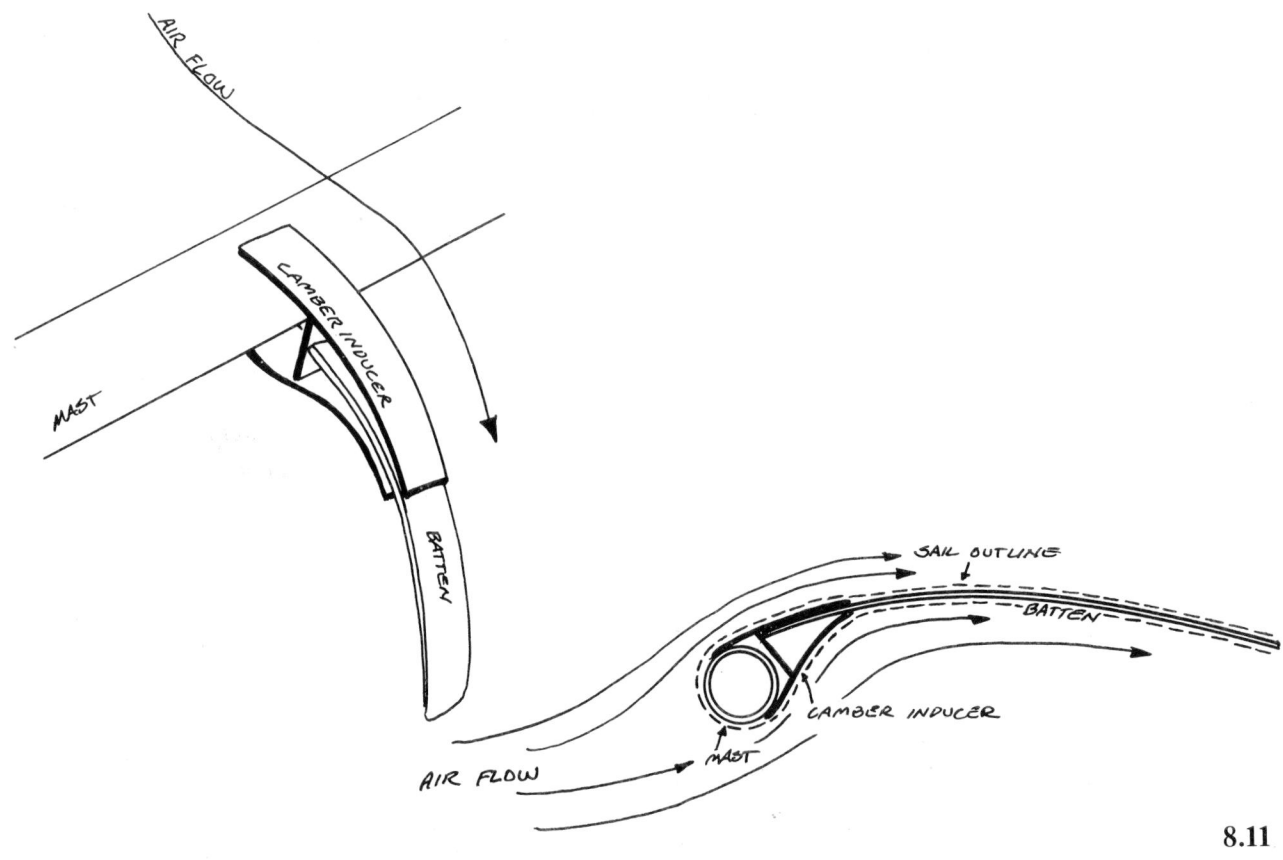

8.11

cent more efficient, I have found that I can carry 20 percent less sail than I would normally carry in any given wind if I were using my standard setup. As a result, Barry has shortened the booms without a visible loss in overall power, leading to a more maneuverable board under all conditions. The only drawback with these sails, as with other fully battened sails, is that they don't luff as nicely as soft sails do, i.e., you can't turn them into the wind and make them flutter to get rid of power in an instant. Still, these are much more powerful and efficient sails. So if speed and jibing is your thing and not tricks or fancy sailing, then the RAF sail is the way to go.

Camber Induced Sail

Like the RAF, a camber induced sail is inspired by the wing mast theory. These sails provide a very clean entry from the mast all the way back to the point of maximum draft. Plastic cambers are inserted between the mast and battens to force the sail to rest to leeward, making for an airplane wing-type foil! These sails are not too fun to sail, but they are proven faster than conventional sails on the race course (Figure 8.11).

Masts

You could have the best-cut sail available, but if it is set on the wrong mast, you'd still be "out to lunch." This is because mast bend greatly affects sail shape and because the curve that's cut into a sail needs to conform to the curve of the mast when it's bent. If there's too much curve in the sail for a given amount of mast bend, then the luff of the sail will be much too full. This keeps a board from reaching maximum speed, as well as from pointing high into the wind. You can easily detect this problem by watching for vertical wrinkles in the sail just behind the mast (Figure 8.12). However, if there's too little curve in the sail for a given amount of mast bend, then the luff of the sail will be too flat, resulting in a loss of power. A too-flat luff produces diagonal wrinkles between the mast and clew (Figure 8.12A).

Sometimes these problems can be dealt with by adjusting either the downhaul or outhaul (covered in Chapter 1); however, there's absolutely no way to get a properly made sail to work on the wrong mast, or vice versa. The best way to avoid such problems is to purchase both your sail and mast from the same reputable dealer, one who knows exactly which sails work best on which masts. Keep in mind, though, that most high-aspect rigs require stiff masts for optimum speed and acceleration.

Mast Construction

Mast construction is just as important as mast bend. At present, the only mast section able to withstand the rigors of sailing in the surf is one that's constructed from a combination of fiberglass and epoxy. Such a mast provides the stiffness necessary to retard the loss of power and control, yet it's strong and flexible enough to take fairly severe pounding in the surf. Polyester is much more brittle than epoxy and therefore cannot take as much stress before breaking. But there are some good polyester masts on the market.

Presently, aluminum and carbon fiber masts are used by many racing sailors and some nonracing sailors who seldom sail in the surf. Such masts are very stiff, making it possible to hold near perfect sail shape for maximum performance. At this time, however, it's not a good idea to go out into the surf with either an aluminum or carbon fiber mast. The aluminum mast will bend or kink at the first good wipeout, and the carbon fiber mast will simply snap, as carbon is also a very brittle material. Both masts are also too stiff for wave sailing.

8.12   8.12A

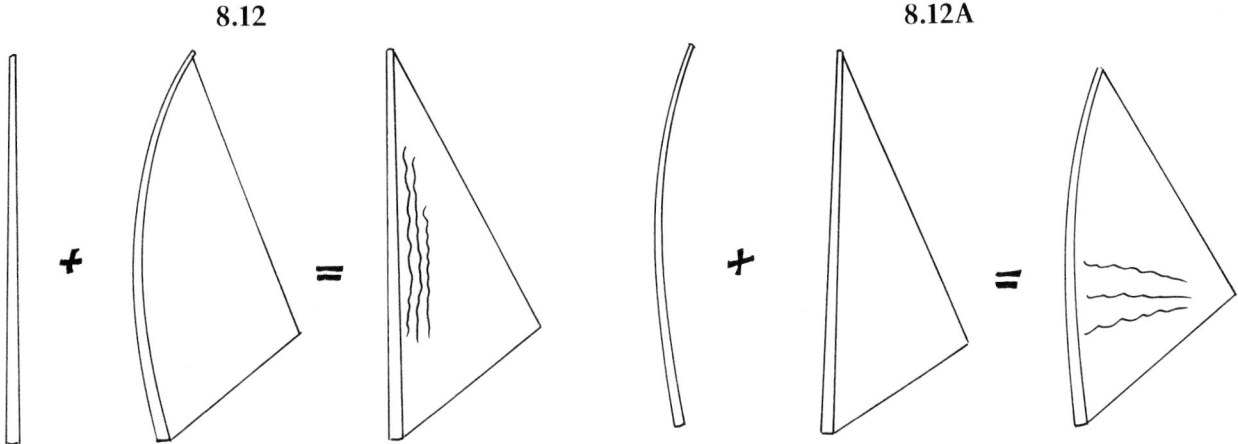

Mast Extensions

Since many performance sailors have two or more sails to accommodate various wind and water conditions, mast extensions are essential. They enable you to use a variety of sails on the same size mast and still keep your clew in the proper spot so that it doesn't drag in the water when you're turning in the surf or rest too high when you're not. Basically, there are two types of extensions in use today. Some are what might be called "add-ons" (Figure 8.13), and others are the "adjustables" (Figure 8.13A). The standard add-ons come in a variety of lengths, but the smallest one you can buy is six inches. The adjustables are simply a longer piece of aluminium tubing with holes drilled through them every four inches or so, enabling you to make quick adjustments by sliding the collar up or down and reinserting the pin. The advantage with the adjustables is that you can set your clew wherever you desire. In fact, I have holes on my adjustable universal every two inches so that I can make very fine adjustments to the height of my rig. The problem with the add-on extensions is that they tend to get jammed with sand and are then hard to take apart or put together. The problem with the adjusta-

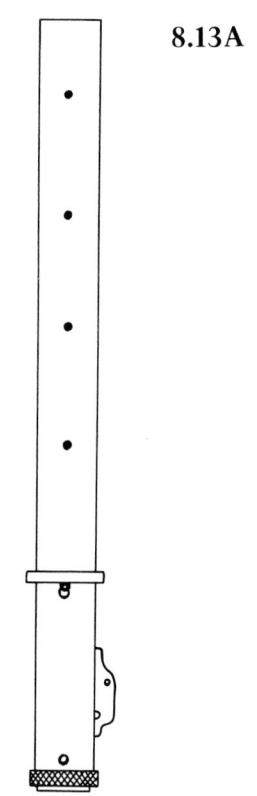

8.13A

ADJUSTABLE MAST EXTENSION

bles is that they tend to bend after a while due to the fact that they are so long and have holes in them for adjustment (for more on clew adjustment, see Chapter 1).

When purchasing extensions, make sure they fit your mast, your other extensions, and your universal (some universals even have built-in extension rigs). The best way to do this is to bring these items along when you go to buy the extensions. In this way, you can make sure everything fits and avoid wasting time and money.

Choosing a Mast Track

When choosing a track, be sure to purchase one that's at least ten inches long, and make certain that it's built to last. If you're solely a performance surfer, with no intentions of sailing upwind a lot, all you'll need is the standard skeg-box setup (Figure 8.14). On the

8.13

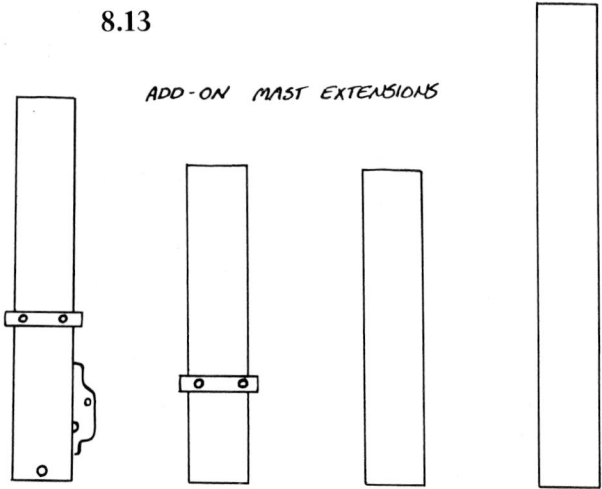

ADD-ON MAST EXTENSIONS

8.14

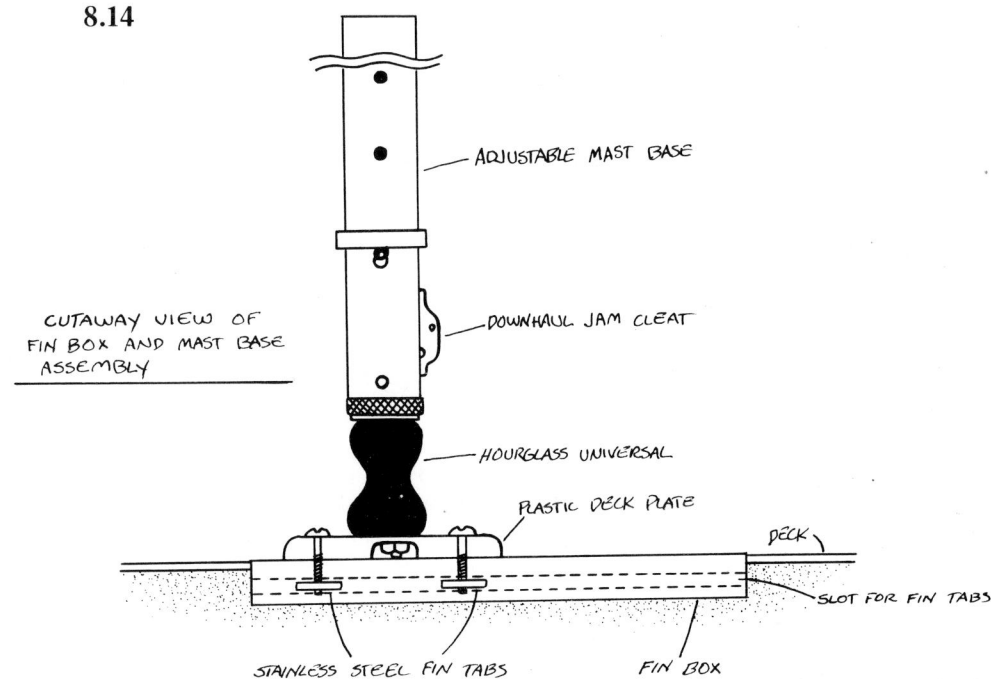

ADJUSTABLE MAST BASE

DOWNHAUL JAM CLEAT

CUTAWAY VIEW OF
FIN BOX AND MAST BASE
ASSEMBLY

HOURGLASS UNIVERSAL

PLASTIC DECK PLATE

DECK

SLOT FOR FIN TABS

STAINLESS STEEL FIN TABS

FIN BOX

other hand, if you do plan to sail upwind or race a lot, you may want an on-the-water, adjustable mast track. With one of these, you can decrease wetted surface for offwind sailing by moving the mast aft, or increase wetted surface for upwind sailing by moving the mast forward. Many good mast tracks, of all types, are on the market. I suggest you ask your dealer and fellow sailors for recommendations, but I must admit that I really feel that adjustable mast tracks are unnecessary for recreational sailing. I have never felt the need for one myself.

Universals

Numerous universals are presently on the market, and many of them are good. The main thing to look for in a performance universal is strength, since performance boards are constantly under tremendous loads. In this regard, aluminum universals seem to hold up far longer than those made primarily of plastic. Of the swivel types, the Windsurfer universal has long been a proven performer and can be mounted into any number of deck mounts. Rubber and/or nylon universals swivel as well as most other types, but they do tend to break more easily. The problem here, of course, is that a breakdown can mean

you will have difficulty getting back to shore on your own. Another good universal we'll be seeing more of is the rope universal. If the rope breaks, it's easy to repair right on the beach.

If you windsurf a lot, however, no matter what type of universal you have, you are likely, at one time or another, to experience a "universal breakdown" (not to be confused with the collapse of a black hole in the far regions of the cosmos). For this reason, I recommend that everyone buy a universal with a safety line that attaches its base to its top. This way, even if you have a breakdown you can "jury-rig" a universal with the safety line and sail back to shore, however slowly.

With so many advances taking place on a daily basis, again, I can only recommend that you speak with other knowledgeable sailors or your dealer in order to find the universal best suited to your needs.

Universal Mounts

Currently, two good universal-to-board mounts are available, although custom, adjust-while-sailing mast tracks normally have their own special mounting car and track setup. However, most custom fiberglass boards have the skeg-box rig and come with either one of two types of mounts, both of which use screws and skeg plate sliders that fit into the box. One is a rectangular plate with two screws, one on either end used to tighten the plates onto the board and to allow for adjustment and removal with a screwdriver (Figure 8.15

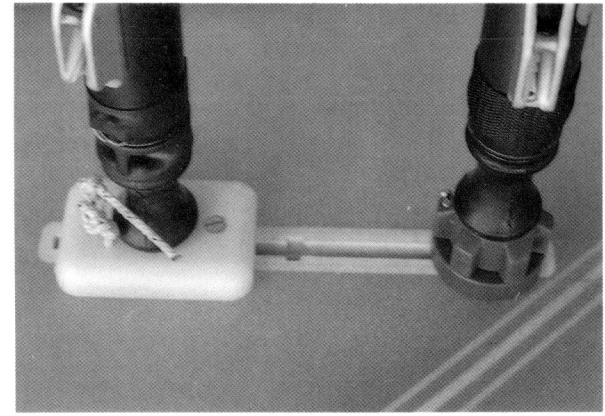

8.15

at left) The other is a triangle or round-type plate that has a single screw securely mounted into the plastic. This screw is adjusted or the mount removed simply by turning the entire base plate of the universal. Since I prefer to use as few tools as possible, I really like this system.

Booms

Choosing a boom is a pretty straightforward affair. The best are made with thin-walled aluminum (but with at least 59/61 tensile strength), have the narrowest wishbone you can handle while still allowing for sufficient curve in the foot of the sail, are as stiff as possible, are anodized, and have a coating that promotes good grip.

For performance boards, adjustable booms are excellent. An adjustable boom enables you to lengthen or shorten your boom so that you can accommodate a number of different sails and their varying foot lengths. Two adjustable boom types are currently popular: the telescopers and the add-ons. With both types, you may get some water leakage (more so with a telescoping rig) and a little flex, but not enough to worry about.

The telescoping types are advantageous chiefly because you don't have to carry a lot

of different extensions around. But if you don't rinse the boom out with fresh water from time to time, it could freeze up and you'll no longer have an adjustable boom. The add-ons are longer-lasting and less likely to freeze up. The only drawback is that you have a couple of pieces of extra equipment to worry about.

Boom Ends

There are plenty of fine boom ends on the market. Choose whichever one you feel has the most solid construction, is compact, has a 3:1 or 4:1 pulley system, and has few moving parts. Also, the front end should fit snugly to the mast and be easy to tie and untie. My suggestion is that you get one that's guaranteed by the manufacturer. If the manufacturer won't guarantee it, you'd be making a mistake to put any confidence in it yourself.

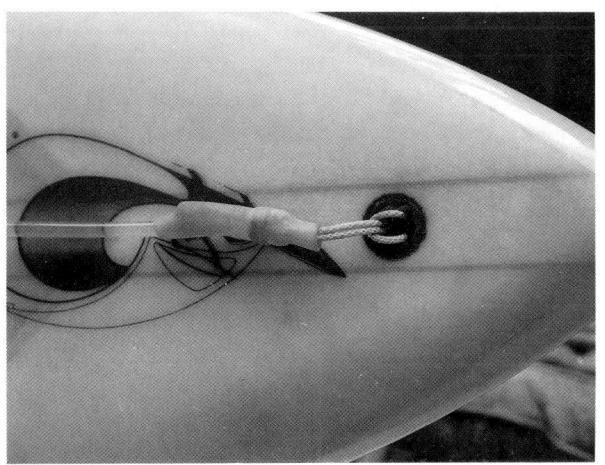

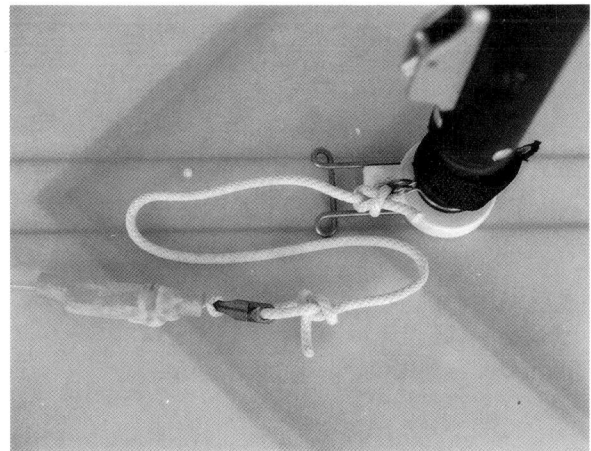

8.16

8.16A

Leash

Attaching a leash to your board's mast is essential if you plan on surfing or sailing far from shore in that it ensures that your board and sail won't get separated in the event of a wipeout (Figures 8.16–A). The best place to anchor the leash is the board's nose. A leash anchored here keeps the board's bow pressed against the wave so that it offers the least possible resistance to passing white water.

For safety's sake, you'd be advised not to sail far from shore without a leash. Already we have lost several sailors in various parts of the world because they lacked common sense. For although I can't be certain how all of these sailors were lost, I don't doubt that

some were lost from not having leashes. Here in Maui, I regularly see windsurfers being driven down the coast by someone who picked them up after they swam ashore. They then have to search the downwind shore for their leashless board. In most instances they do find it, but what they fail to consider is what would happen if the wind were blowing offshore and they lost their board far from land. It's a question easily answered: Unless you can swim upwind against the current, or are lucky enough to be rescued, you are likely to lose your life. Certainly it's a foregone conclusion that you'll also lose your board.

8.17

Daggerboards

Many performance boards in the nine-to-twelve-foot range are manufactured with a retractable daggerboard (Figure 8.17). On a pure wave-riding machine, a daggerboard simply isn't necessary. However, if you plan on sailing most of the time on flat water and won't be surfing a lot, having a daggerboard will increase upwind performance at little cost to reaching performance—as long as it retracts completely into the hull. In winds of more than eighteen knots, though, a daggerboard is seldom needed, unless your're trying to point high into the wind when facing a current. Since there are many fine daggerboard systems currently on the market, I suggest you do some asking around to find the one that will suit your needs best. However, always go for quality—a little extra cash spent on shore often means a lot more pleasure out on the water.

Harnesses

8.18

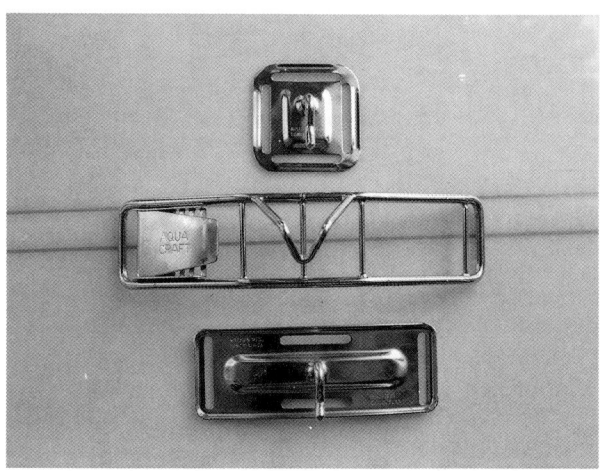

A number of good harnesses are on the market. The best as far as durability is concerned are those made with U.S. materials—be wary of Asian brands unless you are certain the materials were made in the United States.

Some harnesses are light but not very buoyant for wave-riding purposes (since you need to dive deep if you get caught inside during a big set), while others are thicker and well padded—some are even Coast Guard approved as PFD's (personal flotation devices). I always prefer a low back harness for support and comfort. Hooks range from small to medium to full spreader bars (Figure 8.18). I prefer small hooks, but spreader bars, while bulky, are more comfortable and better for your ribs and lower back. Be wary of plastic hooks, although not all plastic hooks break.

Footstraps

Most performance boards come to you with footstraps already in place, and if you purchased your board from a reputable builder, chances are they'll have been positioned and mounted properly. Small performance boards (those under eight and a half feet) generally need only three or four straps: one or two aft (for various planing speeds) and two forward (for your forward foot when sailing on either a port or starboard tack). When the board is longer than eight and a half or nine and a half feet, it's sometimes necessary to add extra straps forward for sailing when the winds lighten up (Figure 8.19). Board balance is always affected by where you stand on the board.

Spend the extra money for a strap that's comfortable and won't stay crushed when you

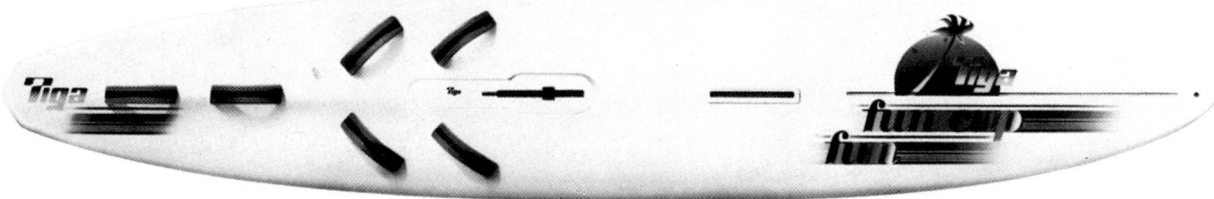

into it. It's well worth it in the long run. I prefer an adjustable Velcro strap, but beware of cheap Velcro that wears out quickly.

The greatest danger presented by footstraps is the possibility of a wipeout at high speed with your feet stuck in the straps. Like falling out of control down a ski slope with bindings that won't let go, you risk breaking your ankle or leg. To adjust the straps properly, first decide whether you want to sail with boots on or barefoot. Then, adjust each strap so that it covers the area just behind your toes. If your straps are set up so that they release under pressure, give them a good tug on shore to see whether they come undone. If you can't undo them with a mighty heave, they need to be loosened; if they come undone with just a moderate pull, they need to be set more tightly.

Nonskid

Having a good nonskid surface on the deck of a performance board is essential.

Several types of nonskid are currently popular for performance boards: nylon peel-off, foam dust, wax, nonskid tape, and spray-on traction.

Nylon peel-off is a type of nonskid that only fiberglass board manufacturers are able to use. They simply laminate nylon or fiberglass cloth onto the board and peel it off before the resin dries. The resulting imprint leaves a nicely textured, nonskid surface.

Foam dust is also a type of nonskid generally used only by fiberglass manufacturers. What they do is spread a layer of resin over the board's deck and sprinkle foam dust on it before it dries. After the resin is dry, you can sand the dust to obtain any grip texture you want. I prefer this type of nonskid because, in my opinion, it provides the best traction. Some sailors use a variation on this theme by substituting either salt or sugar for foam. Salt gives a very good grip, but it's so gritty that if you fall on your board you can get cut. Sugar is good, too. The only problem with using sugar is that ants love sugar decks—if you leave your board alone in the yard too long, you're bound to start a colony.

Some sailors like to leave their decks glossy and wax them as needed with a professional surfboard wax in order to get good traction. Wax works fine, but it can get messy, since it melts in the sun. It's also rather unattractive and requires constant reapplication.

Various nonskid tapes, such as Astrodeck and Action Traction, are also popular with windsurfers. These tapes provide good grip, but add a little more weight than other nonskid tapes if used over the entire board. Two advantages with nonskid tape are that it comes in a variety of colors for decoration and in a range of thicknesses, such as in rad pads (Figure 8.20), which serve as padding for your feet under the footstraps. Such padding also helps to prevent pressure dings on the deck of your board when you're jumping a lot.

Spray-on grips, such as Griptons, are also good for nonskid. To get the grip you want you simply hold the can at various distances away from the board as you spray on the nonskid. The closer to the board you spray, the smoother the surface you get. The farther away you spray, the grittier the surface you get. And if you don't like the surface you've sprayed on, you can sand it down to make it smoother. All in all, spray-on grips work pretty well.

Summary

As you can see, buying performance equipment involves a lot of choices. In fact, before you're through purchasing everything you need, you'll probably wish I'd just told you what to get so that you could be done with it. However, I didn't do this for two very important reasons.

First of all, performance sailing is currently experiencing rapid development in construction and equipment technology. The setup I tell you to buy today might not be the one to buy six months from now. That's why the only practical way to deal with this situation is to learn the fundamental requirements for any piece of equipment and keep yourself informed by reading windsurfing magazines and by discussing any changes you read or hear about with other knowledgeable sailors and dealers.

The other reason I haven't provided you

with absolute specifics is that equipment must suit personal needs. What I need and use on Maui may not be necessary for someone sailing in Europe or Asia or California or New York. Also, as I said in the previous chapter, so much of what you buy depends on the kind of sailing you do—not on the kind you dream of doing. If you're going to be sailing on Lake Michigan, for example, you might do fine with a polyester mast, a retractable daggerboard, and a well-made dacron sail. But if you're going to be powering out through the lineup on the Gulf Coast, you'll need a very different setup.

So my advice is to be practical. Buy a setup that suits your needs, not someone else's. And if you can afford to buy top quality, do so. In the long run, a well-made product usually turns out to be the better bargain.

9. Safety

In general, windsurfing is a safe sport. When you consider all of the sailboards in the world and the numbers of fatalities that occur each year, the safety record is outstanding. Of those who do get hurt or are lost, the common factor leading to the accident was a lack of common sense combined with an unwillingness to heed the basic rules of safety.

If you follow the basic rules of windsurfing safety wisely, you'll greatly decrease the dangers of this already very safe sport. Here they are:

1. Don't go out in offshore winds unless you can handle them and rescue is close at hand. If you get tired, or something breaks down, you'll be blown out to sea.

2. Check the weather forecast so you're prepared for what's to come. If a storm is brewing, stay close to shore.

3. Learn about the tides and how they affect your local sailing area and surf spot. At some places, certain tides present dangers that cannot be ignored.

4. Choose the right sail size for the conditions. It's not good to get stuck on the water with too much sail in a blow, or very pleasant to be out with too little sail, especially if the wind drops so much that you have to paddle in.

5. If you go out, the wind drops, and you cannot get to shore under sail, you'll have to paddle in. To do so, sit on the board, detach the rig, and push it out to windward until you can untie the sail at its clew. Then roll up the sail as tightly as you can from the bottom to the top, making sure to tuck the battens away carefully so you don't rip the sail. Now, tie up the sail to the boom with the outhaul or downhaul line. Finally, lie down on the board with the mast and sail underneath you or resting on your back held by your legs and paddle to shore (Figure 9.1). And no matter how far from or close to shore you are, never leave the board.

9.1

6. Cold water and wind can bring on hypothermia, the leading cause of death in water sports. Never underestimate the need to keep warm with wetsuits. So dress up, not down, and before you're really pooped out, sail in.

7. If you can't swim, you probably shouldn't be windsurfing and certainly shouldn't go out in waves since you can't dive under them after a wipeout with a life jacket on.

8. Check your gear before you sail. If anything is likely to break, repair it. If you use a harness, always carry a spare harness line.

9. If your universal is not permanently attached to your board and there is any chance of the mast separating from the board, use a leash.

10. Never sail alone. And if you sail offshore with a friend, tell someone to keep an eye on you. If you go for a long-distance sail to another destination from where you started, call someone when you arrive to tell them you made it safely. If you don't call, then they know you're in trouble and can arrange for help.

11. Learn the basic right-of-way rules that govern the waters, especially if you sail in crowded areas where all types of boats are around. The five most important ones are as follows:

A. Starboard tack (Figure 9.2). This is the golden rule of sailing: starboard tack has the right of way over a boat on port tack. When the wind is blowing over the starboard side of a boat, that boat is said to be on a starboard tack. The boat on the port tack must stay clear.

B. Overtaking (Figure 9.2A). A boat coming up from the rear must stay clear of the boat ahead. You can pass another boat on either side, just be sure to give the boat you're passing plenty of room.

C. Head to wind (Figure 9.2B). When two boats are approaching each other head on, each boat must stay to the right.

D. Give way to larger boats. If you're out sailing in the harbor and a freighter is heading up the channel, give it plenty of room. This only makes sense since the motor yacht is difficult to maneuver in a restricted area. The "power gives way to sail" rule does not apply where there is a great difference in size and maneuverability.

12. Never, under any circumstances, abandon your board. The only time to let go of it is when you're on shore, bailing out from a jump, or stepping up onto a rescue boat. Your board is your lifeboat—leaving it is usually a mistake.

13. Never stay hooked into your harness when jumping, unless you're only skipping small chop.

14. If things get out of control during a jump, bail out: push your board to leeward and dive to windward. Then grab your board as soon as possible.

15. Always stay between your board and oncoming foam. The foam is powerful, and getting hit by your board is no laughing matter.

16. If you're down in the surfline and getting hit by large waves, grab the tip of your mast and sink it as far as you can.

17. If you wipe out, try to fall so you don't hit the bottom. This is especially important if you're surfing over a coral reef (or a granite ledge).

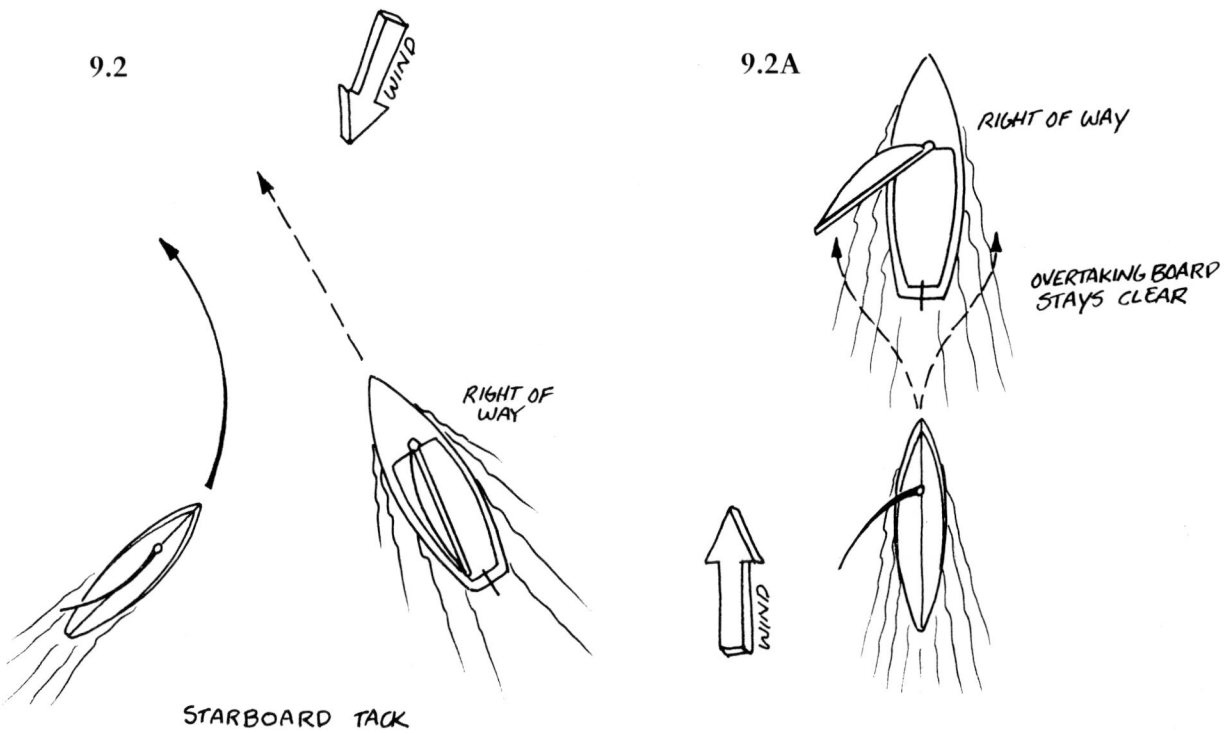

9.2

WIND

RIGHT OF
WAY

STARBOARD TACK

9.2A

RIGHT OF WAY

OVERTAKING BOARD
STAYS CLEAR

WIND

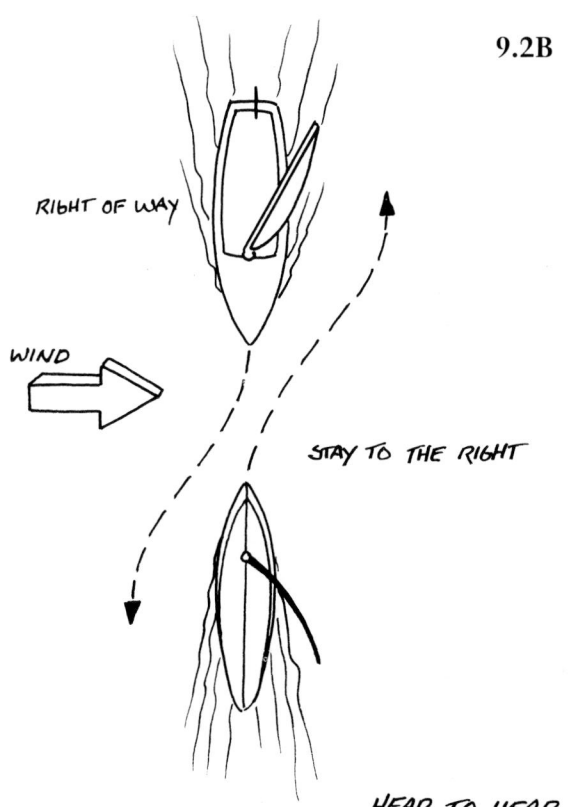

9.2B

RIGHT OF WAY

WIND

STAY TO THE RIGHT

HEAD TO HEAD

9.3

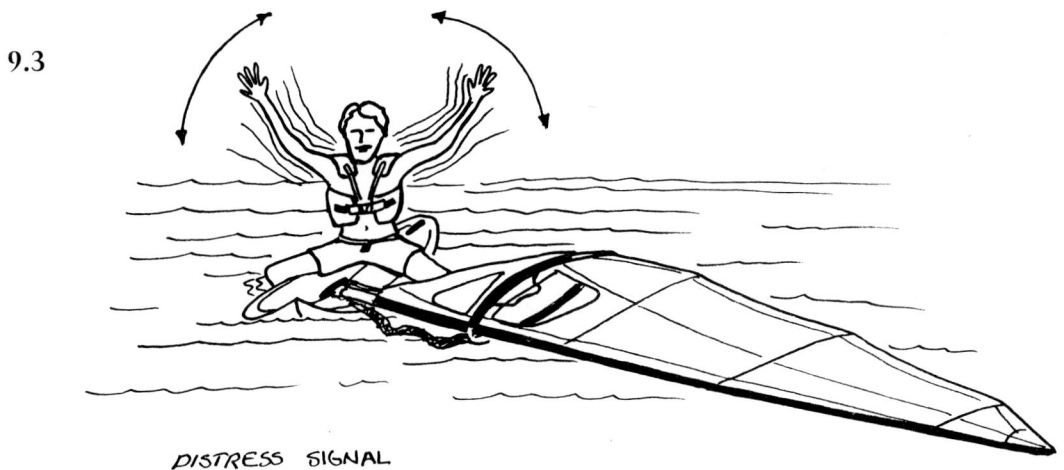

DISTRESS SIGNAL

18. Always tie your board to the top of your car carefully. If it flies off you risk hurting others as well as damaging your board. This is no joke.

19. If things get bad and you can't paddle to shore or come up with any kind of jury rig, sit up on your board and wave your arms from side to side (Figure 9.3). This is the international signal for distress, and so long as you do it properly, anyone who sees you should know you're in need of help.

20. Coral cuts should be washed out with hydrogen peroxide as soon as possible. Then they should be treated with an ointment such as Neosporin and bandaged. A better way to prevent cuts is to wear protective footwear, in the form of rubber windsurfing shoes.

Play it safe, have a good time, and get RADICAL!

Glossary

A

Abeam— A position reference. Any object bearing at right angles to a board's keel line is abeam.

ABS or ASA— Plastic material from which production boards are manufactured.

Aft— A position reference toward a board's stern.

All-around board— A board that can be used in a wide range of conditions. A board that is versatile.

Apparent wind— The vector (change in direction) produced by a board's forward speed. The wind one experiences on a moving board.

Aerial— To hop off the face of a wave and then come back down on the same face while still maintaining control.

Aspect ratio— The relationship between a horizontal and vertical dimension. A tall mast and short boom make a high aspect ratio sail plan.

B

Backside— To sail across the wave with your back to its face.

Backwinding— Holding a board's sail out toward the windward side to slow it down.

Bailing out— To leave your board when in danger of a wipeout. This is done by taking your feet out of the straps and pushing your board to leeward.

Batten— A thin, narrow strip of fiberglass used to stiffen up the shape of a board sail.

Beach break— A type of surf break where the waves break close to the beach on sandbars, as opposed to reefs or rocks.

Beam— 1. The width of a hull. 2. At right angles to the centerline of the board.

Beating— Tacking the board back and forth to gain distance in a windward direction.

Blank— A large block of foam from which a custom board hull is shaped.

Bottom turn— A turn made at the bottom of a wave to project the board back up the face toward the lip.

Bouncing out— Same as bumping out.

Bow— The forward part of a board's hull.

Bowling up— A section of a wave that is breaking all at once and in a very tubular fashion. Board surfers turn into bowls for tube rides, but sailboarders need to go around them since they can't fit entirely inside the tube.

Broad reaching— Sailing with the wind aft of abeam.

Bumping out— Losing control of the tail because you are moving too fast for the thickness of the tail for your weight and can't sink it in enough to get the rails to bite.

C

Carve— Turning the board sharply on its inside rail.

Caught inside— Getting stuck inside the surfline due to a wipeout or a set of waves that are just too large to power out through.

Cavitation— When air is drawn down the side of the skegs, causing them to lose contact with the water.

Centerboard— A movable fiberglass fin that can be raised or lowered through the keel of a board's hull. The centerboard imparts stability and helps to prevent leeway.

Chop— Short irregular waves used for jumping.

Clew— The aft corner of a sail.

Close out— Collapse of a long section of wave.

Custom Board— A hand-shaped and hand-glassed performance board made exactly to the specifications of the buyer.

Cutback— A turn made off the top of the wave or down on the shoulder used to turn the board back toward the breaking wave.

D

Daggerboard— A removable unpivoted keel.

Dead downwind— Directly to leeward.

Deck— The top of the board upon which the rider stands when sailing.

Downhaul— The line attached to the tack of the sail used to put tension on the luff. On performance boards, the downhaul needs to be set very tightly at all times.

Draft— The degree of concavity to a sail. Camber depth.

Drawn out— A long, wide turn.

Drilled— Getting pushed to the bottom or pummeled in the surfline after a wipeout near the impact zone.

E

Ease off— To let out the boom a bit. To fall off the wind by turning down.

Eating it— Just like getting drilled, but can also be used to describe a bad fall or nose pitch.

Eye of the wind— The exact direction from which the true wind is coming.

Extensions— Aluminum sections used either to lengthen or to shorten a mast or boom for a particular sail or rider.

F

Fall off— To alter course away from the wind. To fall off the board when sailing.

Fathead— A sail with a very wide head that needs to be supported with battens.

Fenced fin— A fenced fin helps to stop cavitation by keeping the air bubbles that originate near the fin base from getting out to the tip.

Fiberglass— Material used in board construction. Fiberglass allows for a very light and stiff board, but one that is more fragile.

Flare— Either sinking the tail of a long board in a jibe, or kicking the back of the board into the wind on a jump.

Flat— A term used to connote a flat sail, or one with very little fullness.

Flex— Measurement of the degree of bend in boards, booms and masts. In general, less flex makes for more speed, but this is not always the case.

Floater— A standard board, or a performance board which you can uphaul without sinking in any amount of wind.

Foil— The thickness of a skeg or fin in the cross-section. Normally, maximum foil thickness rests about one third back from the front of the fin or skeg.

Footstraps— Loops of webbing or plastic used to help the rider stay on the board when turning, planing, jumping, or surfing.

Foot— The bottom edge of a sail, extending from the tack to the clew.

Frontside— Riding a wave with your chest facing the curl.

Full— A term used to connote a full sail, or one with a good deal of concavity.

G

Gak— A big-egoed sailor who talks better than he sails.

Geek— Like a gak, but less extreme!

Getting air— Very similar to an aerial.

Glide around— A smooth turn carried out with the momentum built up by a board prior to turning.

Gnarly— Dangerous or frightening conditions.

Grommet— A metal ring set into material for a line to attach to or through.

Gun— A narrow high-speed board.

Gust— A sudden increase in wind velocity.

Gybe— Same as jibe. Complete a change of tack with the leech of a sail passing through the eye of the wind.

H

Harness— Accessory designed to take the strain off the sailor's arms. It is strapped to the body with a hook positioned near the chest. This hook is then set in a line attached to the boom of the board, and the rider leans out using the harness for support.

Haul— To pull in.

Head— The top of the sail.

Header— A shift of wind coming more toward the bow, forcing the rider to fall off or sheet in to maintain proper sail trim.

Head up— To alter course toward the wind.

Hitting the lip— Driving up the face of a wave and timing things so that the nose of your board smacks the lip and then gets thrown back down the face with incredible speed.

Hull— The board itself, without sail or rigging.

I

Inconsistent— 1. Surf conditions with infrequent sets of waves. 2. Sailing conditions with up and down winds.

Inhaul— Line attaching the boom to the mast.

Induced drag— Drag caused by eddies along the foot and head of a sail.

K

Kevlar— A special ICI fiber, derived from a type of nylon. Kevlar is stronger than fiberglass and lighter for its weight. Kevlar is also very expensive.

Kick out— To get out of a wave before it ends or closes out.

Knots— Nautical miles per hour. A nautical mile is longer than a standard mile: nautical mile = 6,060 feet; standard = 5,280 feet.

Kook— A kook is the ultimate gak!

L

Lacerating— A term used to describe a sailor who is really cutting up the waves. A lacerating surfer is one who is often radical but not smooth. This is the rock and roll style of surfing as opposed to the jazz or concert style.

Late drop— A waverider who drops into a wave at the last second, when it is very steep and just about to break.

Lamination— The joining of layers of fiberglass or some other material to another. In board manufacturing, the fiberglass is laminated to the foam blank. In sail construction, dacron is laminated to mylar to give it tear resistance.

Leading edge— The foremost edge of a sail.

Leash— A line used to attach the rig to the board. A great safety item.

Lee— To the side opposite from which the wind is blowing.

Leech— The after edge of a sail, running from the clew to the head. The leech is normally kept from flapping by battens inserted into the sail.

Leeway— The board's sideways drift due to wind pressure. Leeway is reduced by using a daggerboard, especially upwind.

Lift— A shift of wind more toward the board's stern, enabling the rider either to head up or to sheet out.

Lip— The breaking part of the wave at the top.

Locals— Those who have lived and surfed at the same spot for a long time. Locals are to be given extra leeway in the surf because you are stepping into their territory.

Luff— The area of the sail that runs parallel to the mast.

Luff up— To alter course toward the wind so the board slows down.

Lull— A brief dying of the air.

M

Marginal sail— An all-weather sail.

Mast foot— The part that attaches the power joint to the board.

Mast rake— Positioning the top of the mast fore and aft in relation to the straight up and down position.

Maxi— A large sail for light airs or heavy riders.

Mushy— A slow breaking wave that crumbles down from the top.

N

Nose— The front of the board.

O

Off the wind— 1. Sailing at a wide angle to the wind. 2. Reaching or running.

Off the lip— Same as hitting the lip.

Offshore winds— Not good for surf sailing.

One design— An organized class of sailboards that are identical in design and organized for racing.

Outhaul— A line that holds the clew of the sail to the boom. When tightened, the outhaul serves to flatten out the sail.

Over the falls— Getting sucked over the back of the wave and then on over to the foam. Not fun! You usually get pounded.

P

Peak— The spot at which the wave first begins to break.

Peaky conditions— Waves breaking in all different directions.

Pearling— Sticking the nose in and getting pitched over the front of the board. Happens mostly when trying to get up on a plane or when hit by a gust. When surfing, happens when you're dropping in too late or with your weight too far forward.

Peeling— A perfectly shaped wave with a lip that breaks evenly from the peak all the way toward shore.

Piece of chop— A breaking section of chop which can be jumped.

Pinhead— A sail with a narrow roach at the top.

Pitching— A lip that throws out a great deal, forming a very hollow section in the wave.

Pivot— A turn which is not drawn out, but made in a very tight arc and mainly off the tail. The ultimate pivot turn is done when performing a scissor jibe.

Plane— Sailing over the water with a minimum amount of hydrodynamic drag. Smoking!

Planshape— The overall outline of a sailboard hull.

Pointing— Sailing as close to the wind as possible.

Polyethelene— A thermoplastic board hull construction method, either roto-molded or blow-molded.

Pop a wheelie— Lifting the nose of the board to ride over foam in the surf, similar to lifting up the front wheel off a bike to ride up and over a curb.

Pop-out— A plastic board as opposed to a custom fiberglass board.

Port tack— Wind coming from the port side.

Pounded— Getting pushed around by the foam after a wipeout, oftentimes, all the way to the bottom.

Power joint— A rubber joint attached at one end to the mast base and at the other end to the mast foot.

Puff— A sudden burst of wind that is blowing stronger than what is blowing at the time.

Pumping— Manipulating the rig to create wind in the sail and make the board go faster, or to help it hop up onto a plane.

R

Radical— 1. A very powerful or difficult wave-riding maneuver. 2. Rough or gnarly conditions.

Rails— The sides of the board.

Reaching— When a board sails with the wind abeam or slightly forward or aft of the beam.

Reef break— A surf spot where waves break over a reef.

Resin— A petroleum substance used to cover fiberglass to make it hard and strong.

Rig— Mast, sails, booms, and all the gear needed to make them work under sail.

Rip— Current caused by waves or tides. Can be seen as short, confusing chop. To get out of a rip, swim sideways to the shore.

Ripping— A waverider who's got it all under control and who is turning radically and smoothly.

Rocker— The amount of upward curve in the nose and tail of a sailboard. More rocker creates a more maneuverable board; less rocker, a faster board.

Running— When a board sails dead before the wind.

S

Section— A long shoulder section of a wave that's about to break all at once.

Scoop— Curvature of the nose.

Shaper— The craftsman who shapes foam blanks into sailboard hulls.

Shorebreak— Waves that break almost right on the beach, impossible to wave-ride.

Shoulder— The part of the wave that has yet to break.

Shredding— Like ripping or lacerating.

Sideslip— 1. Drifting downwind as opposed to making headway upwind. 2. spinning out.

Sinker— A board that won't support the weight of the rider unless it is moving very fast. A board that cannot be sailed in light air.

Skeg— A fin or fins positioned at the tail of the board to give it stability and prevent it from spinning out at high speeds.

Slashback— A sort of cutback maneuver, but done closer to the lip and in a sharper arc.

Slashing— Performing really sharp, radical turns, not always smooth and graceful.

Snap— A fast, sharp turn. A snappy board responds instantly and can turn in a pivoty fashion.

Spinning out— Turning the board so sharply that its fin(s) loses contact with the water, allowing the tail to drift sideways. Very common when making bottom turns or fast, carving jibes in heavy air.

Squeezing the sail— Pulling the sail in tightly just before a jump or plane to get maximum power and speed.

Squirrelly— A board that turns very easily and loosely. A board that can pivot fast off the tail.

Stall— A breakdown of aerodynamic forces, usually caused by separation of air flow on the leward side of the sail. An oversheeted sail is a stalled sail.

Starboard— Right side, when facing forward.

Stern— Back of a board.

Stoked— A person that's excited about the sailing and or wave conditions.

Sucking up— A section of the wave that is very steep and hollow and powerful.

Surf— To ride a wave on a sailboard.

Surf rat— A sailor who lives solely for wave sailing.

T

Tacking— Turning the nose of the board through the eye of the wind to change tacks.

Tail— The aft section of a board.

Tearing— Just like lacerating, ripping, etc.

Thruster— Tri-fin setup on performance board.

Top turn— A turn made at the top of the wave to bring the board back down the face.

Tracky— A board that is the opposite of squirrelly, one that likes to go straight, like a car set up with very tight rack-and-pinion steering.

Trim— To adjust sail angle for perfect aerodynamic efficiency.

Trimming— Setting the sail perfectly and riding the board near the middle of a wave to get maximum speed and sideways distance so the rider can make it around a section of a breaking wave.

Tripping— Catching the rail of the board on a wave face, which often makes the rider fall off or slow down drastically.

Trough— The hollow between two waves.

True wind— The wind that would be present in the absence of the board and its movement.

Tube— A very hollow wave.

U

Upwind— Toward the wind.

W

Waterstart— Method of starting a sinker. The sailor lies back in the water and lets the wind in the rig pull him to his feet.

Wetted surface— Area of a board's hull in contact with the water.

Wind shift— Change of wind direction.

Windward— Facing the wind.

Wipeout— Falling off the board, normally in the surf.

Wired— A sailor who understands the conditions and sails in them well.